The Secret of the Singing Heart

Abridged Edition

C. W. Naylor

WARNER PRESS

Anderson, Indiana

The Secret of the Singing Heart: Abridged Edition, by C. W. Naylor, copyright © 1930, 1954 by Warner Press, Inc. All rights reserved. For permissions and other editorial matters, contact:

Communications and Publishing
Church of God Ministries, Inc.
PO Box 2420
Anderson, IN 46018-2420
Toll-Free: 800-848-2464

To purchase additional copies or obtain distribution information, contact:

Warner Press, Inc.
PO Box 2499
Anderson, IN 46018-2499
Toll-Free: 877-347-3695
Web site: www.warnerpress.com

Unless otherwise noted, all Scripture quotations are from the King James Version of the Holy Bible. Scripture references and other text that did not appear in earlier editions of this book are enclosed in brackets [ ].

ISBN   1-59317-128-5
        978-1-59317-128-5

Printed in the United States of America

05 06 07 08 09 10 / UG / 9 8 7 6 5 4 3 2 1

Contents

Preface

"Oh, why did not someone tell me sooner?" wrote a woman who had passed through some very trying spiritual experiences. It had been my privilege to explain some of the difficulties to her. She experienced great relief of mind and spirit by coming to look on her troubles in a new light.

About the same time, another person wrote, "If I had known these things thirty years ago, I might have been spared much and my life thereby made far happier than it has been."

Hundreds of such letters through the years have convinced me of the need for a book dealing with these experiences, which are common to so many of us.

It is my purpose here to point out some of the underlying principles of Christian life. I hope to make clear the way into the joyfully victorious life, so that the reader may walk life's way with the "everlasting joy" that belongs to those who have learned *the secret of the singing heart.*

—C. W. Naylor

The Fountain of Song

The whole earth is at rest, and is quiet: they break forth into singing. —Isa. 14:7

Nature is joyful. Song wells up from the heart of the world. We have heard of the music of the spheres. A harmony makes itself heard above the discords of earth. This world is not a place of melancholy. Its drab colors when properly blended become beauteous. Its discords may be merged into harmonies.

Happiness is the normal state of all life. Our tears are meant to be only the cleansing rain which refreshes and beautifies life. There is an echo of far-off music in all the sounds of nature. Rejoicing is everywhere. Happiness is God's will for all his creation. "Sing, O ye heavens . . . shout ye lower parts of the earth: break forth into singing, ye mountains, O forest, and every tree therein" (Isa. 44:23).

This universal joyfulness is also thus expressed, "The valleys . . . shout for joy, they also sing" (Ps. 65:13). Again, "Let the nations be glad and sing for joy" (67:4). In nature sentient beings are happy even though life for them is full of danger and hardship. The birds sing even though they know they are surrounded by enemies. Constant dangers do not silence their songs. In spite of all the cruelties of fang and claw, and undeterred by storms or cold, hunger or privation, the voice of joy still rises in melody.

In man likewise pulses the same joyfulness. Difficulties may come, dangers may surround him, he may make failures, suffer losses, and sometimes almost despair. Notwithstanding all this, any normal person will rise superior to his difficulties, and the song of joy will not be fully quenched. Troubles, when they lie

5.

in the past, may be quickly forgotten. Trees bent over by snow rise again when the snow is melted, to gaze anew upon the sun. So man rises from his troubles. He lifts his head up into the sunshine, and again his heart breaks forth in joyfulness. The heart is naturally merry, and God would have it ever so. "My servants shall sing for joy of heart" (Isa. 65:14).

While preparing to write the chapters that follow, I took my concordance and Bible and looked up some of the words that express rejoicing and happiness, such as rejoicing, gladness, happy, blessed, joy, rest, etc. I found these words and others of similar import nearly nine hundred times in the Scriptures. Even then my search was only partial. Assuredly this multiplicity of joyous expressions should convince us not only that happiness is the natural state of man but that it is God's will for him.

Again and again we are exhorted to rejoice, to be glad, and to give expression to our joy. The poet has said, "Hope springs eternal in the human breast." Joy is more powerful than sorrow. Peace is more lasting then trouble. Sorrow is but transitory. Life has balm for all our woes, light for all our darkness. Morning breaks after the darkest night. The sun shines after the fiercest storm. Spring's warmth and beauty return after the cruelest winter. In the normal life happiness is the rule; unhappiness the exception. Troubles will come. There are misfortunes to be endured, but these need not take out of life its beauty, its happiness, or its worth.

One conviction should ever be present with us. Our happiness does not depend upon our environment, our station, our circumstances, or any external thing. The songs come from within. They bubble up out of the heart.

There's no defeat in life
Save from within;

Unless you're beaten there
You're bound to win.

It is what we are within that counts—our outlook
on life, our purposes, our ideals, our hopes, our faith.
There are joyful beggars. The most thankful, the most
appreciative, are often those who have little. Some of
the most contented, cheerful, and lighthearted people
I ever saw were people whose situations seemed least
tolerable. In my ministry I have gone into homes
where poverty abounded, where sickness and sorrow
existed, yet I found in some of those homes happy,
trustful, rejoicing hearts. Favorable external circumstances may encourage the song in the heart, but the
lack of these things need not still the song. External
benefits alone cannot produce a song in the heart. A
favorable condition of heart is like the reed of the
wind instrument. The wind itself can produce no
music without the reed. So the music in human hearts
is born in the soul. As the reed in the instrument
makes the instrument vocal, so the proper qualities
in the heart make joyous music even in the night of
sorrow.

Too many people have a wrong philosophy of life.
The pessimist makes his own clouds. The optimist
sees the sunshine on the other side of the clouds and
is happy. Some modern idealistic religious systems,
though based on false metaphysics and a false natural
philosophy, have, outside of these, a true philosophy
of happiness and success, at least for the present life.
Many of us could learn much from these philosophies
that would be very helpful. We need not accept the
vagaries of their metaphysics or natural philosophy
nor those of their spiritual concepts, but the hopeful
outlook, the expectation of success, and the discount-
ing of the unpleasant and undesirable is the true way
to happiness. The God who made the birds that sing

so sweetly desires the same melody of song in the hearts of the highest of his creation. Believing this, we face life with the elements that create melody active in our hearts to teach us *the secret of the singing heart.*

A Great Adventure

Life has wonderful possibilities for good or for evil. It may be a great adventure upon which we go, with ever changing scenes through which we may march with our heads up and a song of victory in our hearts. To many life is this. On the other hand, life may mean a servitude in which the weary, discouraged, and almost hopeless prisoner of fate marches on toward an eternal dungeon. One may be a slave to worry, fear, foreboding. Life may be a series of defeats. But this is not the normal life. No one need live such a life.

Life was intended to be triumphant, joyous, prosperous. It was meant to be filled with gladness, with light hearts, and with singing. Facing life as we are capable of facing it we can make it an ever ascending pathway with our vision taking in ever remoter horizons. Life may be a series of discoveries. Each day there is new territory to be explored, new experiences to be had.

The terrain of our life is largely of our own choosing. We may go on the upland way or down through the swamps. We may enjoy the fragrance of flowers and of fruit, of pines and cedars, or we may endure the miasma of decaying vegetation. Life is full of boundless possibilities. It is a great continent lying before us awaiting exploration. Shall we go through it with bowed heads and burdened shoulders, or shall we cast off our burden, lift up our heads, and act like men and women in the midst of a great adventure?

Explorers do not always have an easy time. Frequently they have great difficulties to overcome. But exploration gives zest to life. The constantly changing scenes always bring fresh interest. The difficulties and privations of the past are quickly forgotten in the inspiring prospect that lies before us. We need to cultivate the spirit of the explorer. We need to develop our possibilities and capabilities and to have the inspiration of a great purpose.

It is easy to say, "Oh, I do not amount to anything; I never can be anything; I never can do anything worth while," and then settle down in the prison house of this attitude and never be free, not because we might not be free but because we do not choose to be free. So often people say, "My life is not worth living." Every life is worth living, and every life is worth living right. Too many lives are like an airplane so heavily loaded it can never gain altitude.

We must rid ourselves of some burdens if we would live a normal life. A bird entangled in a net cannot fly. It must first be freed from its entanglement Our entanglements are often of our own making. We build our own prisons; we shut ourselves up in our own cells. Circumstances can never long imprison us if our spirits are free. "Stone walls do not a prison make, nor iron bars a cage." The free spirit cannot be imprisoned. Let us not be content with servitude. Let us cry out with Patrick Henry, "Give me liberty," and then strike with the sword of a determined will to cut our way through whatever may imprison or hamper us. Do you say, "This is easier said then done"? True, but it can be done by everyone. It is well within the possibilities of each of us.

What are we getting out of life? In the first place, we can get out of it no more than we put into it. So if we are getting too little out of our lives, if they are unsatisfying, or impoverished, or hemmed in, it is because we are putting too little into them. Our lives are what we make them. It is not how long we live but how intensely we live, how full of worth-while interests we fill our lives, that makes them satisfying.

Life in reality is what we are within. Circumstances are the casket in which lies the jewel of personality. The value is not in the casket but in the jewel. Therefore, life is not made up of favorable or unfavorable circumstances, nor of possessions either many or few, nor of recognition or the lack of it, nor of honors bestowed by others. It is what we are that gives quality to all these values. We can blend musical sounds to produce either harmony or discord. Things can be made either helpful or harmful.

Chemical elements can be combined to create either wholesome or poisonous compounds. Whether we have happiness or unhappiness depends upon the elements we put into our lives and how we combine them. If we put into our lives selfishness, disregard of others, unkindness, discourtesy, ill-temper, complaints, murmuring, distrust, doubts, fear, hate, malice, envy, covetousness, and the like, we shall inevitably suffer bitterness, dissatisfaction, and sorrow as the natural result. Let us not say that God makes our life as it is, or that it is our lot, or that people wrong us.

No, we are making the quality, if not the form and outline of our lives. Circumstances alone neither make us nor mar us. It is our reaction to circumstances that produces results in us. What ruins one makes another. To some, obstacles become stumbling stones, but to others, steppingstones, according to the use made of them.

So after all, what we shall have in life is our own choice. We are the architects of our own lives. If we build with noble materials, carved with patient care, we shall have beauty and grace. If we put into life love, loyalty, gentleness, meekness, kindness, faith, forbearance, patience, hope, we shall not fail to draw good dividends from all these, dividends which will, rejoice our hearts, cause our eyes to sparkle and the song of gladness to well up.

The purpose of life is not merely to have a good time, to gratify the senses, to eat, drink, and be merry. Its high and holy purpose is the building of character. Good character is the basis of real happiness.

> *Only the holy and innocent sing*
> *Out of a bosom where pleasures abide.*

The process of character building is not always easy, but it is always profitable. Each of us has capacity to develop strong character, a noble and beautiful life which cannot be unhappy. Such a soul has depth into which trouble can never reach. No matter how trials and troubles may press in, a calm and undisturbed peace holds the center of such a life. Joy springs up on the darkest days. Light shines in the deepest night. Life must have its disciplines and its difficulties to make it of value, to give it character. Iron ore is of little value until it passes through the fire and is purified, tempered, and shaped. The chisel must bite deeply into the marble again and again before the angel in it looks out. Likewise disciplines, seemingly valueless or even hurtful, bring riches greater than a king's ransom when the soul accepts their training.

The Christian life of many people is unsatisfying. Instead of being joyous it is burdensome. There are two causes for this. If when we come to God we still cling to the past and try to graft Christianity onto our old lives, we cannot enjoy the fruits of righteousness. We must break with the past. We must find a new life. We must become new creatures. With the old life that is forsaken will go many of the causes of heartache and sorrow and burden. However, if when we come to God we give up many things that have gone far to make up life for us but do not replace these with something better, we impoverish ourselves and our lives become barren and unsatisfying.

We should fill our lives with the pleasant deeds and thoughts of righteousness, of truth, and of service. These make life rich for ourselves and profitable to others. We need the freshness and beauty of true spirituality. We need activities and interesting and profitable fellowship.

God said, "Rejoice and be [exceeding] glad" [Matt. 5:12]. The Christian life is full of wonderful possibilities. I do not mean a formal and empty Christian profession. I mean the inner divine life begotten by the Holy Spirit. A life spent in exploring the kingdom of God on earth is always an interesting, attractive, and happy life.

Let us make our lives a great adventure. It is our privilege now and then with heart and mind to make an excursion to heaven, there to sit and meditate beside the river of God. We can go back through history and become acquainted with the saints of old. We can have fellowship with their joys. We can drink of the rivers of pleasure and eat "honey out of the rock" [Ps. 81:16]. We can live love's way; bask in the sunlight of heaven. We can "run and not be weary, ... walk and not faint" [Isa. 40:31].

Five Kinds of Religion

Christianity is a singing religion. The coming of Jesus was ushered in with the joyful chants of the heavenly throng. Singing has ever been a prominent part of the worship of God. When the soul has a vision of the God revealed in the New Testament it is uplifted, illuminated, inspired, exalted. This exaltation naturally bursts forth into songs—songs of joy and true happiness.

The vast wealth of song written by Christians and used in their religious devotions is in a strange and almost startling contrast to the lack of song in the other religions of the world. Music has little part in the worship of other systems of religion. The American Indian may sing his war song or song of the chase in his religious festivals. The votaries of other religions may also sing, but these are generally not songs of worship or attempts to express their own joyfulness in the service of their gods. Rather such songs are usually efforts to placate the gods. It is true that Buddhists in some countries are borrowing the Christian custom of song in worship and are adapting Christian hymns to their worship. It should be noted, however, that this is a mere adaptation in the face of Christian competition rather than an original part of Buddhism. So Christianity may be said to be the only singing religion, except, of course, the worship of Israel, from which it was in a great measure derived.

Religion has a powerful influence upon happiness. It adds much to, or takes much from, natural happiness, according to the kind of religion one has. Christians do not all believe in the same sort of religion. True, they all believe in one God and in one Bible and in a general way in many of the same teachings. When we come to practical religion, however, there are about five kinds of Christian religion. Four of these produce little happiness; in fact, they may hinder happiness. They may stifle the song that would naturally arise from the free heart. The reader will do well to pause to consider which, if any, of these five kinds of religion he has, or whether he has a mixture of them.

First, there is the *don't* religion. It is the religion of self-denial. It is hedged in with numerous restrictions. It is a religion in which the worshiper is kept in a strait jacket. It is largely a negative religion. Persons having this kind of religion may be very strict, very sincere, very earnest, but they never can be truly happy. Happiness never comes from purely negative attitudes. When we deny ourselves anything, the purpose should not be merely that we be without it, but that we may put in its place something that will contribute more to our own or others' happiness and well-being.

Religion is intended to make people free, with the highest type of freedom. "If the Son therefore shall make you free, ye shall be free indeed" [John 8:36] is the essence of the New Testament. A *don't* religion is conducive to bondage. Such negative religion offers a sort of satisfaction. It may gratify the sense of duty, but we must get a different sort of religion in order to know *the secret of the singing heart.*

The second kind of religion is the *do* religion. It consists of merely following forms and ceremonies, or obeying rules and regulations, or doing works of merit. Its followers may find considerable satisfaction in reading prayers, in bowing down and rising, in making the sign of the cross, keeping holy days, making pilgrimages, following rituals, and going through forms. Some of the forms of religion have a certain value in helping to produce correct emotion, but they are a poor substitute for the realities of true religion. Formalism may be accompanied by stately singing, grand organs pealing forth, and intellectual discourses, though the heart of genuine religion may be absent. The esthetic sense is grati fied while the soul is left unfed or perhaps impoverished. This do religion trusts in works. It draws much satisfaction from what it has done. A religion of mere works, of forms and ceremonies, can bring little true happiness.

Another form of religion is the *Sinai* religion. It hedges in its followers with "thou shalt" and "thou shalt not." It is the mere keeping of commandments. It is a worshiper of authority. It is doing because one must. It is refraining from doing for fear of punishment. The God of Sinai still thunders forth in this religion. He is a great and awful God, crowned with majesty and glory, but far removed from the worshiper. He is worshiped in fear and trembling at the foot of the mountain whose summit is hidden in angry clouds. Out of these clouds flash the lightnings of divine vengeance. It is a stiff and rigorous religion. There is little of grace or mercy in it. It is walking by rule. There is little in it to start the songs that come from a peaceful and happy heart.

Then there is what may be called the *slippery* religion. It is one that people must hold fast with all their might lest it slip away from them. People who have this type of religion are constantly in fear of losing it. If they do this, or that, or the other thing, they wonder, "Now, have I lost my religion?" They are always examining themselves. They are always questioning and wondering. They cannot for long settle down to certainty. They are often overwhelmed with doubts and fears. They are constantly observing their emotions to see whether or not these emotions indicate whether they still have religion or have lost it.

Perhaps they pray and earnestly try to draw near to God. Then if joy and happiness come, they are satisfied and sure they have their religion. But presently a dark day comes. Their emotions subside. Then they wonder again whether they still have their religion. In reality their struggle is not to keep their religion, but to keep their emotions and to satisfy their own questionings and doubts. This religion carries them alternately to the mountaintop and to the depths of the valley of humiliation. It is truly an "up-and-down" religion. The slippery sort of religion can never be the source of true and lasting happiness.

The fifth and true type of religion, the religion that corresponds with the teachings of the New Testament and with the experiences of those who have learned the way of Christ is *the religion of the heart*. It is not a religion of restriction, neither of formalism. It is neither Sinai religion, nor slippery religion. It is a religion in which the heart is in its natural element. It is a religion of peace and contentment, a religion of joyful service. It is the natural expression of the soul. It is a peaceful and harmonious relation with God. It is the relation of a child and its father. Its elements are trust, simplicity, sincerity, purity, faith, love, and all the fruits of the Spirit. It is a Spirit-filled life. All these attitudes and relations are the deep sources that feed the bubbling springs of joy that flow forth in rejoicing and song.

In this sort of religion God is not a great and terrible monarch, a stern judge, a taskmaster; nor are his laws a set of hard decrees. No, the Christian religion as seen in its true light is "good tidings of great joy...to all people" [Luke 2:10]. It is written, "Happy is that people whose God is the Lord" [Psa. 144:15]. With such a religion we not only read of the joys of salvation in the Scriptures but have the experience of them in our own souls. In this sort of Christian life we do not fear God in the sense of being afraid of him. We do not tremble before him. Godly fear becomes the equivalent of reverential love. Out of divine and spiritual love flow even greater joys than flow out of natural love.

Real religion has two sides. First is the inside—the relations of the soul with God. The Scripture says, "Acquaint now thyself with him, and be at peace" [Job 22:21]. That means to get acquainted with God, get on good terms with him. Know his goodness. Come into close contact and association with him. To know him thus is to be at peace with him. We must have the inner experience of divine life in the soul and union with Christ. This is open to everyone who will seek it in God's way.

The other side of religion is the outside. There can be genuine outside religion only when there is genuine inside religion. James defines the outside of religion by saying, "Pure religion and undefiled before God and the Father is this, To visit the fatherless and widows in their affliction, and to keep himself unspotted from the world" (1:27). A pure and holy inner life issues in a pure and blameless outer life, devoted to service and helpfulness. This is the religion that is a well-watered land, full of fruitfulness. It is a land of song and cheer and of true blessedness.

The Christian life is the life of the "new song." When the psalmist looked back upon the "horrible pit" and the "miry clay" out of which the Lord had delivered him he cried, "He hath put a new song in my mouth" (40:3). The Revelator saw the great host of redeemed souls gathered before the throne of God, and he said, "I heard the voice of harpers harping with their harps: and they sung as it were a new song before the throne" (Rev. 14:2–3). Chapter 15:3 reveals the nature of this song, "And they sing the song of Moses the servant of God, and the song of the Lamb." The song of Moses was the song of Israel's deliverance from Egypt and their enemies after the crossing of the Red Sea. The song of the Lamb is the song of salvation. So the song we sing is a song of deliverance and of salvation. No wonder it is a joyful song!

The song has a special characteristic. "No man could learn that song but the hundred and forty and four thousand, which were redeemed from the earth" (Rev. 14:3). This company of people, represented in symbol by the "hundred and forty and four thousand" [Rev. 7:4], are all the redeemed of God. The song that could not be learned by others was the song that is learned only by experience, the experience of redemption and salvation through Jesus Christ. It cannot be sung by mere professors of religion, nor by formalists, nor by legalists. It breaks forth only from the hearts of those who are happy and free in Christ.

Isaiah, foreseeing this glorious age of salvation, cried, "The ransomed of the Lord shall return, and come to Zion with songs and everlasting joy upon their heads: they shall obtain joy and gladness, and sorrow and sighing shall flee away" (35:10). This is the experience of those who have learned *the secret of the singing heart*.

The Worry Tree

The black walnut tree has a peculiar quality that affects the soil about its roots with a poisonous substance very unfavorable to the growth of many kinds of vegetation. Some grasses may grow under it, but many other plants shrivel and die.

Something in many lives corresponds to the black walnut tree. In its baneful influence the good life cannot develop.

This noxious tree grows in the land of unbelief. It is found nowhere else. It is the worry tree. Many lives are cursed with this tree. It is one of their most prominent characteristics. It spreads its shadow over everything. It shuts out the sunlight. It poisons the soil. It draws up into itself the resources of the soul as a natural tree draws water from the soil, leaving spiritual faculties and powers parched and impoverished; it prevents their proper development and fruition.

Worry is one of the worst attitudes that can come into a life. Perhaps only sin is worse; worry may even become sinful. It is a form of fear. Fear, worry, anxiety, foreboding, are all the same in effect and will here be treated together. The worry tree does not grow in the land of faith. But in the land of unbelief and questioning it spreads its great roots of doubt deeply into the soil. The results of worry are too numerous to be recounted in full.

One result is that wherever worry is given place it stops the song of joy. We cannot be glad when we worry. We cannot be free and happy. The moment we worry peace, joy, satisfaction, comfort, all vanish. The sun goes behind a cloud. A chill wind blows. Many people make themselves utterly wretched through worry. Its effects are not merely spiritual. The whole being is poisoned by it. Perhaps it would be well to consider some of the effects worry produces. If we know those effects it may help us to avoid their causes.

We note first the physical effects. Certain glands that control the bodily functions are excited to action by fear. They secrete a powerful substance that is poured into the blood stream and produces immediate effects. It is this that enables one to run faster when danger threatens or to expend greater energy then than at any other time. A good purpose is served by these glands, but when they are constantly over-stimulated by fear, worry, anxiety, or any other emotion they produce too great an effect upon the nerves. This tends to make one nervous, and nervousness in turn reacts to produce fear and worry. This action and reaction continued, repeated over and over, break down the nerves. A great many nervous people are what they are simply because they have given way to worry. It upsets the whole course of nature. Many physical disorders are the direct result of worry. A few quotations from medical authorities may help to make this plain.

Dr. [George W.] McCoy says, "The mind can have a powerfully stimulating effect toward either health or disease. When the mind is properly used and controlled health may be maintained under many adverse conditions, but when the mind is torn by conflicting, destructive emotion, it kills the very cells it is supposed to guard over and control." Again he says, "You must realize how important the mind is as a factor in the production of many chronic disorders. Sometimes this process is so insidious as to be unrecognized except by the closest attention of a skilled diagnostician. In my practice I have seen a number of cases of paralysis which were induced by slight injury associated with fear. Although these patients had been to many different doctors and undergone many different kinds of treatments they were not cured until this fear factor was recognized, and then the cure took place almost instantly."

Dr. [Royal Samuel] Copeland, once health commissioner of New York City, says, "Worry has pronounced effect upon the organisms. The digestion is upset because the nerves controlling the circulation and muscular structures are "jumpy" and disturbed in function. The intestinal action is disturbed. The brain and nervous system are upset. The glands operate irregularly. The whole system is deranged. Good teeth, as indeed good eyes and ears and heart and blood vessels and liver and kidneys, are dependent on lack of worry and plenty of restful sleep. Worry is deadly to vigor and usefulness."

A whole book of this sort of quotations could easily be selected. Dr. G. H. McIntosh says, "If men could wipe out all fear from their minds, nine-tenths of them would be free from sickness." Henry Ward Beecher said, "It is not work that kills men; it is worry. Worry is rust upon the blade."

The mental effect of worry and fear is just as great as the physical effect. Through worry people often work themselves up into, a sort of mental fever so that their nerves "go to pieces." When we worry the mind cannot think clearly. The judgment is impaired. Minor difficulties seem out of proportion. They do not seem natural, but appear altogether different from what they do when the mind is in a normal condition. Sometime worry produces great mental distress. Sometimes it partly or entirely unfits one for work. Have you not heard people say, "I am so upset I just cannot do anything"?

This mental condition reacts upon the body; the physical effects of worry react upon the mind; and we have a vicious set of actions and reactions set up, destructive alike to mind and body. An agitated state of the mind affects the brain tissues. The poison created in the body through fear and worry reacts upon the brain tissues and the mind becomes still more troubled. These things are not imaginary. They are being suffered by thousands of individuals. People get up in the morning tired out. They have no energy. They have to drive themselves. This is one common effect of worry. Another common result of worry is lack of mental control so that the mind cannot be concentrated on anything.

Worry also has a spiritual effect. It destroys faith. In fact, faith and worry are mutually destructive. Faith will destroy worry and worry will destroy faith. So whichever is given ascendancy will destroy the other. Worry stimulates doubts. The more we worry the more we doubt. We have heard people talk about blind faith. Faith is not nearly so blind as doubt. Doubt cannot see favorable circumstances. It sees everything in an unfavorable light and magnifies it. There may be ever so many favorable elements in a situation, but doubt sees none of them. Worry sees none of them. Worry brings gloom and discouragement. It makes one moody, forgetful of God's goodness and mercy and helpfulness. In fact, worry shuts God out of the picture. It causes us to forget him or makes us doubt him, ourselves, and others. Under the influence of worry we can draw the most gloomy mental pictures. We clothe everything in somber shades.

Worry also leads to self-condemnation. It makes us minimize the good there is in us and the good there is in life. It prevents us from exercising our powers. With worry there is a great troop of evils. They cluster around it and add to its damaging influence. Worry is always evil. It never serves any good purpose. It never aids us in accomplishing anything. It never makes anything easier. It has nothing to recommend it.

More than that, *worry is never necessary*. Mark well that statement. It is a positive truth. Worry is never necessary. First, it never can help us. It can never make things easier or better. It never did any good. It never cured any trouble. Second, we do not have to worry. There is always a better way. We shall attempt to point out that way later.

Worry is altogether folly. It not merely does no good—it always makes matters worse. It weakens every good thing. It strengthens every bad thing. Worry is a noxious tree. It bears poisonous fruits. Have you one of these poisonous worry trees? You must rid yourself of it before you can sing the glad songs of rejoicing that come from a free soul. One of the secrets of the singing heart is the remedy for worry.

Fruits of the Worry Tree

"Self-preservation is the first law of nature." Everything has some method of protection. Even the plants have "defense mechanisms." Animals have shells, teeth, sharp claws, are swift of foot or wing. Some of them produce noxious odors. Some of them are unpleasant to the taste. The octopus secretes an inky fluid with which to color the water. Some animals have great skill in hiding themselves. Some have electric defenses. Some are covered with spines.

Man has a natural instinct of self-preservation. He will run or fight or secrete himself or use other methods of defense. This law of defense is manifest in man's physical contact with nature. This is known too well to need explanation. He has also various mental defense mechanisms. Likewise in spiritual things he seeks to protect himself.

These various defense mechanisms have a powerful effect upon our conduct. When we are brought into a trial, threatened by something that will hurt or annoy us, when we are afraid, our defense mechanisms begin at once to function. The first impulse is to run away, to escape from the trouble. We shrink from what hurts. We try to avoid trials and all hard or unpleasant things.

It is often the part of wisdom to avoid unpleasantness as far as we can without sacrificing something vital. But if we give way too much to this disposition to shrink and run away we shall become cowards. We lose strength of character, courage, and the qualities that win in life. A coward can never feel self-respect, and if we are spiritual cowards we shall be lacking in manhood and womanhood. We cannot respect cowardice even when it is in ourselves.

This disposition to escape unpleasantness often leads to an unfair excusing of ourselves when we have been at fault. It often leads to our putting the wrong face on happenings, to exaggeration, to minimizing of the facts, or even to plain lying. These are the natural fruits of fear and worry, and they undermine spiritual character. They take the joy out of life. We need to watch our defense mechanisms and be sure that we use right methods of defense, methods that build up the character rather than tear it down; methods that increase courage, faith, and determination. We should conquer the instinctive cowardice of our natures. "Safety first" may be a good slogan, but safety through the measures mentioned is not real safety. It is only exchanging one kind of danger for another.

Another defense mechanism is the tendency to resistance. When we adopt proper measures of resistance the results will probably be good. We are likely to be strengthened, encouraged, and helped. It is likely to bring out the best there is in us. But sometimes this instinct of resistance manifests itself in murmuring, complaining against circumstances or against people, blaming others for our plights or our troubles, shifting responsibility. These may become chronic fault finding and result in such a critical attitude that we are hard to please, contentious, ill-tempered. We may become disposed to impatience and find it hard to practice self-control. We may harbor resentment against others and become unkind and uncharitable in our attitude.

Not only do non-Christians have such trouble, but many Christians are tempted in this way. They worry and fear. They become discouraged, and then the characteristics mentioned begin to manifest themselves in them. They have a fight to overcome them. They wonder why they are impatient, why it is hard to be kind, why they feel resentful.

They need not be surprised, however. The impatience and resentment merely indicate an effort to escape from some unpleasant situation. So you need not be surprised if you find conflicts within when you worry and give way to discouragement. To get rid of the conflicts get rid of your worry, your fear, and your discouragement. Then the tensions will naturally disappear. But if you are given to worry do not expect to escape wholly from tenseness and conflict. Indeed you are likely to have much trouble with them. These are not necessarily the result of sin. They are the result of worry and fear. They come from a wrong attitude of mind, a wrong outlook on life, a wrong way of trying to overcome difficulties.

In such a situation the outlook is negative. We need to change to a positive attitude. We need to put faith in the place of doubts. Trust instead of worry. Look on the bright side instead of the dark side.

A negative attitude destroys our faith and robs us of courage, so we can bear little. It covers the bright picture of hope with sackcloth. It banishes peace. Instead of soul rest we have turmoil and trouble. It robs us of balance and poise. Confidence fades away. It gives place to distrust. We lose our power of initiative. In fact, worry and fear rob us of all the choice blessings we might possess. They prevent us from using our powers and make us pigmies instead of giants.

The triumphant life results from courageous action, and courageous action is always based on faith. It has a hopeful outlook. It faces the future with confidence. This is the normal attitude of the Christian. But worry causes heaviness, discouragement, dissatisfaction, despondency, and perhaps despair. Long giving way to worry will change the character. The blithe gaiety of childhood, the courageous strength of manhood, the joyful song of victory, give way to moroseness and gloom. Clouds cover the sky and we forget that the sun shines anywhere. We ruin our influence with others. They feel more like shunning us than being in our society. Worry shackles our hands. It robs life of what is most worthwhile. If we cultivate a worry tree or a number of them we must expect they will bear this sort of fruit.

Worry also has another extremely bad result. It dishonors God. We say God is our Father, that he is taking care of us. We say we have faith in him. We say we believe God is faithful. Then we act in a way. altogether contrary to this faith. If God is our God and if he is taking care of us, if we are safe in his care, if no evil can come to us without his permision, then what are we worrying about? If God really is what he says he is and what we believe he is we have no reason to worry. Things are bound to come out all right. God will find some way to bring us through to victory. He will work for our good in whatever life may bring. If we really believe God is true and that he is true to us, there is not a reason under heaven for us to spend one moment worrying.

Again, worry dishonors God's Word. He has made definite promises. These promises are true or they are not true. If they are not true then we may have cause for worry. But if they are true let us act like it. Do we actually believe God's Word? If, so, when we are tempted to worry let us sit down, take that Word, and read its promises. Then let us believe them and act as though we believe them. When we do this there can be no room for worry.

Worry ignores the help God has given us in the past and the victories we have won through his grace; also those victories we have won through our own strength. When we are tempted to worry we should sit down and look over the past and see how many circumstances came out better than we expected they would. We should observe how God has helped us in the past and say with one of old, "Hitherto hath the Lord helped us." It will do us great good, when we are tempted to worry, to recount our past victories; to look back and see that our past worries were all for nought. When did worrying help anything for you? When did worrying keep anything from coming upon you that otherwise would have come? When did worry shield you from any trouble? Get rid of your worry tree. Get out from under its shadow. Get into God's sunshine. If you will do this it will not be long until the song of victory flows forth from your lips, and peace and courage and hope spring up anew in your heart.

26. Fertilizing the Worry Tree

Some people are not satisfied to have a worry tree and to permit it to grow as it will. They fertilize it and water it. Oh, no, they do not mean to do this! Nevertheless they do it. They would like to be rid of their worries. Very often they worry over their worries. I once knew a woman who was so given to worry that when everything was going well and she could find nothing to worry about she would worry because she thought things were going too well and would certainly bring trouble. Nor is she the only person of this sort I have seen. But how do we fertilize the worry tree? There are many ways. Some of them we will recount.

First, we increase our worries by failure to face the facts calmly. We are like some horses. We become frightened at some things which have in them nothing that ought to frighten us. When we come to realize this we are sometimes quite ashamed of ourselves. When there is a threatening or unpleasant prospect before us and we are tempted to worry over it we should not allow ourselves to become excited or agitated. We can meet difficulties in calmness better than we can when agitated; when we are masters of ourselves better than when we are the prey of our fears.

We should face the facts—all the facts. We should not merely take note of the ones that oppress our feelings most. Our tendency naturally is to look at the worst side, to be impressed by the most threatening elements, and to overlook the favorable ones. We are influenced by our feelings more than by sound judgment and by our fears more than by our courage. Troubles often look much worse than they are. In fact, we can usually bear them better than we suppose we can, but we are naturally disposed to take one look at any threat, then fear the worst. One of old said, "I feared a fear and it came upon me." Why did his fear come upon him? Because fear made him adopt an attitude that opened a way for its coming. He threw down his shield of faith. He began to tremble and shrink. If he had resolutely faced his fear it probably would never have come upon him.

Failure to give weight to the facts we know will fertilize the worry tree. Very often we know that we can meet trouble if we will. We know there are certain favorable aspects we should consider. But instead of giving attention to these we look entirely at the unfavorable appearances. We forget that the weapons of our warfare are mighty through God. We are like a soldier who told an experience he had in our Civil War. One day he was riding with a comrade when suddenly they came face to face with two of the enemy. There was a lively exchange of shots. In the end one of the enemy lay dead upon the ground while the other was severely wounded.

Upon returning to camp this man examined his revolver. To his surprise not a shot had been fired. His companion had done all the shooting that had overcome their enemies. He had sat on his horse like a statue, forgetting all about his part. I fear all too many of us forget our weapons and the ability we have to use them, and instead of fighting we worry and worry.

Another mistake we make is giving way to our feelings rather than controlling them. Our emotions are easily stirred, whether they be joyful emotions or the opposite. Very often bad feelings assert themselves—

fear, doubts, timidity, foreboding. We give place to them. We let them run riot. We fall into a panic. We should take command of our feelings. We should master them. Our action should be a response to good judgment instead of to our emotions. Many people are tormented by the foreboding of evils to come, and these forebodings are the source of disturbances in all the faculties. This need not be if we will control ourselves and make the intellect rather than the emotions the captain of our soul.

We fertilize the worry tree by exaggerating the possibilities of evil and by not considering the probabilities of good. When we are threatened with some evil let us ask ourselves, "Will this necessarily turn out evil? Will it necessarily prove to be what it looks as though it might be? Will the results assuredly be what they promise to be?" Let us look at the factors that may balance these possibilities. Let us give due weight to the possibilities on the other hand. Let us ask ourselves whether we are not adding to the real dangers by our imagination. Let us see if we are not magnifying the chances of things going wrong. Strip the circumstances of the seeming and get down to the reality. They will usually be found to be much less dangerous than they appear, and we shall see that there is little if any cause to fear them.

A fertile source of trouble is self-pity. I know of nothing that can torture a soul more than self-pity, and this self-pity has in it an element of cowardice. We say, "Oh, it is too bad that I must suffer so. It is too bad that I must have such trouble. How unfortunate I am! How much I have to endure! Why cannot I get along as others do? Why cannot I have an easy time as they have? Why must my way be so rough? Why must I meet so many difficulties? Oh, poor me! What shall I do?" If one wants to make himself thoroughly unhappy let him adopt such a course. It matters not whether there is anything really calculated to produce unhappiness. Self-pity of itself is sufficient. Get rid of self-pity if you want to be happy, for you never will be happy while you have it except for that poor sort of satisfaction which comes through feeling sorry for one's self.

A twin sister to self-pity is a disposition to seek the sympathy of others and to enjoy telling our troubles, magnifying them in a way to excite sympathy. These things shrivel up the soul.

We often increase our fears and troubles by telling them to others. The more we think of them and the more we tell them the deeper the impression made upon our own mind by them.

A further source of trouble is questioning the loyalty of others to us or their interest in us and sympathy for us. Do not expect other people to worry because you worry, or to fear because you fear. Friends are usually as loyal as we deserve them to be. They usually have as much interest in us as we merit by our conduct and attitude. They usually have enough sympathy for us when we actually need it. We should not expect them to have sympathy for us when we are acting in a way that tends to disgust them. If we show ourselves real soldiers and meet difficulty with courageous, hopeful, forward-looking faith, and then circumstances go ill with us we may expect ready sympathy. If we show ourselves cowards, if we whine and sniffle, to bestow sympathy upon us would be to waste it. If we expect others to be loyal to us we must be loyal to ourselves. If we expect them to have an interest in us we must act in a way to arouse their interest.

And finally, we fertilize the worry tree by questioning God's faithfulness, love, and mercy.

Have you been fertilizing your worry tree? If so you have only yourself to blame if it spreads itself over all your dwelling and if it sighs day and night in the mournful breeze, like the somber moaning of the pine.

Destroying the Worry Tree

The vigor and tenacity of life in a tree is determined largely by the soil in which it grows. I lived for many years in a state where the soil is fertile, the ground level, and where beech trees were very numerous. I had occasion to girdle many of them and observed that they were very easily killed. Before that I had lived in another state where the soil is clay and the country very hilly. Here the beech trees were very hard to kill.

I remember a neighbor's attempt at killing a tree that stood by the roadside. Not only did he girdle it, but his boys climbed the tree and cut off the branches a little distance from the trunk. These were then piled around the tree and burned. I wondered why they were taking such radical steps to kill the tree. The next spring I learned the reason. In spite of all this treatment the stubs of the branches that had been cut off threw out new twigs and leafed out. New shoots sprouted up. With all their labor my neighbors had not accomplished their purpose. The difference was not in the climate; it must have been in the soil.

We have already pointed out that the worry tree grows in the soil of doubt. We can hold an attitude favorable to worry and fear. On the other hand we can hold an attitude of faith that is altogether unfavorable toward these things. In order to destroy the worry tree we should change the soil about its roots. We cannot uproot it and destroy it by an act of our will. We can take away its favorable soil. We can develop faith. We can believe in God and in ourselves. We can turn our eyes away from our worries and our troubles and look upon God. We can cease to fertilize the worry tree. We can cease to rob ourselves of our heritage of victory willed to us by our heavenly Father.

We can have that rest of soul God has promised us. We can find it only in him. But as long as we permit all our time to be occupied with giving attention to our worries we shall have no time to give to the cultivation of those graces that God would freely develop in us to give us happiness and contentment. We so often culti-vate doubts instead of cultivating faith. It is important that we learn how we are doing this, and then adopt a different course. We can all have faith if we will go about it right, and faith is the victory that overcomes all our troubles.

One of the best ways to get rid of worries is to ignore the doubts upon which they are founded. Troubles let alone have a way of curing themselves. As long as we fill our brain with worry we increase our trouble. The less we think about our troubles the smaller they become. The more we think about them the more rapidly they grow, and the less capable we are of overcoming them or meeting them successfully.

The surest way to get rid of the worry tree is to cut it down with the ax of faith. There is no worry or fear in trust. If I repeat this thought over and over, it may sink deep into your heart and mind, and that is what you need. When you worry you do not trust. When you trust you do not worry. You cannot do both at one time.

Permit me to suggest a way to develop your faith. Take your Bible and some paper. Write out a list of promises that meet your need. Read these promises over every day. Read them until they become real to you. Whenever you catch yourself worrying or fearing, get those promises and read them. Say after you read each one, "This is true, and it means me." Say this over and over until you come to believe it. Perhaps at first your words will mock you. Perhaps the promises will seem to mock you. I have had the experience. I know how it feels. I know too from personal experience that we can keep right at it, read-ing these promises, asserting that they are true, asserting that they mean us, until in our own consciousness they do come to mean us. They come to soothe and comfort us. They neutralize our fears. Little by little we come to trust in them, and as we trust we cease to worry. Our fears grow less. We come into a restful attitude. There is a sure cure for all of our worries if we take it. That cure is an attitude of simple trust in God and his promises.

Worry is a mental habit. Children are not prone to worry. If they do, it is only momentarily. There is a natural flexibility to the human mind that throws off worry, until we rob it of its flexibility by cultivating the habit of worrying. Any habit can be broken, so the worry habit can be broken. If you are troubled with worry, start in to break yourself of it just as you would break yourself of any other improper or hurtful habit. Worrying is an extremely hurtful habit. It is an abnormal mental state possible of correction, and we owe it to ourselves to correct it.

We cannot help thoughts coming into our minds, but it is within our power to direct our thoughts. We can reject unwelcome thoughts. We can compel ourselves to quit thinking what we do not wish to think. We can supplant improper thoughts with bright and cheerful thoughts. From a long experience of suffering, being confined to my bed with nothing to do, being in fact unable to do anything, and having sunk to the depths of discouragement and black despair, I finally learned to supplant my dark thoughts with bright ones. I found that I must keep my thoughts off myself; so I deliberately turned my thoughts to other persons and ideas. Of course the old gloomy thoughts reasserted themselves, but as often as they came back I supplanted them with something else, and finally broke myself completely of the habit of worrying and of thinking depressing thoughts.

One thing very needful is the will not to worry. Suggestion has a profound effect upon us. Our thoughts have this power of suggestion. We can suggest negative ideas to our minds, or we can suggest positive ideas. We can suggest discouragement, or we can suggest encouragement. We can make our minds run in the channel in which we choose for them to run. Positive suggestion is the basis of a happy and successful life. Make your thoughts help you, rather than hinder you.

One trouble with many people is that they are always resisting something. They are always on the defensive. This attitude of resistance toward our circumstances and surroundings places us under a continuous strain. One writer has said, "Most nervous patients are in a constant state of muscular contraction; but a large percentage of the things that harass and vex them, causing them nervous tenseness, would cease to torture them if they would simply stop resisting. It is our perpetual resistance to annoying trifles that gives them power to annoy us."

I do not advocate surrender to circumstances. What we need is to adjust ourselves to them. This constant revolt against circumstances so common in many people takes the joy out of their lives. It keeps them under a perpetual strain. It uses up their energy to no purpose. Do not use up your energy resisting circumstances. Displace the undesirable by something else if that is possible. If not, adjust yourself to it; make the best of it. Let us use as great intelligence in these matters as we do in others. When I am cold I do not resist the cold; I seek warmth. When I am hungry I do not resist hunger; I seek food. When I am weary, I rest. When I am anxious or worried, I turn to faith and trust. The psalmist said, "What time I am afraid I will trust in thee." He had learned the secret of overcoming trouble.

The word worry is not in the Bible. You may look for it from cover to cover. You will not find it. As God did not think it necessary to use the word worry in the Bible, or have it used there, just so it need not be in the Christian life. To be sure the equivalent is in the Bible. We find fear, trouble, and words of like nature, but we are commanded not to be afraid, not to be troubled.

Many people are like those of whom the psalmist speaks. They are "in great fear, where no fear was" (53:5). The margin says, "They feared a fear where no fear was." Most of our troubles are imaginary, or if there is real trouble we add much to it through our imagination and fear. Some people are so afraid of trouble that they are never at rest. They are frightened [for no reason]; even as it is written, "The sound of a shaken leaf shall chase them" (Lev. 26:36).

Listen to these promises: "Whose hearkeneth unto me shall dwell safely, and shall be quiet from fear of evil" (Prov. 1:33). "He would grant unto us, that we being delivered out of the hand of our enemies might serve him without fear...all the days of our life" (Luke 1:74–75).

The experience of the psalmist may be our experience if we will do as he did: "I sought the Lord, and he heard me, and delivered me from all my fear" (34:4). We shall also do well to hold an attitude like that of the psalmist: "The Lord is my light and my salvation; whom shall I fear? the Lord is the strength of my life; of whom shall I be afraid?" (27:1). The result of holding that attitude is stated in verse 3, "Though an host should encamp against me, my heart shall not fear: though war should rise against me, in this will I be confident." Read also Psalm 46:1-2: "God is our refuge and strength, a very present help in trouble. Therefore will not we fear, though the earth be removed, and though the mountains be carried into the midst of the sea." Again, "In God I have put my trust; I will not fear what flesh can do unto me" (56:4). The exhortation of Christ is, "Be not anxious" (Matt. 6:25, ASV). Read also verses 31, 34; Luke 12:25–26.

Jesus said, "Let not your heart be troubled" (John 14:1). What reason does he give that we should not be troubled? He continues, "Ye believe in God." To him that was sufficient reason for not worrying. It ought to be sufficient reason to us. In verse 27 he says, "Peace I leave with you, my peace I give unto you....Let not your heart be troubled, neither let it be afraid."

Now, for a concluding thought which we shall do well to keep fresh in our minds. When we trust in and obey God, whatever comes to us must come in his will. It must come by his permission. It cannot come without his knowledge. His watchful care is ever over us. He will always keep us no matter how many troubles come. Therefore if we abide in him and his Word abides in us, we shall never have cause to worry. We are safe and secure no matter how threatening future or present troubles may be. So cut down your worry tree with the ax of faith and rest in full assurance of faith in the righteousness and love of God.

Ringing the Joy Bells

Each of us has a large capacity for enjoyment. Some are naturally more exuberant than others. Some are lighthearted and cheerful. Others are sober and thoughtful. Some are emotional. Some are unemotional. Some are inclined to look on the bright side of things, others upon the dark side. But each of us has within joy bells which may be made to peal out the glad tidings of a joyful heart.

Sometimes these joy bells ring spontaneously, but very often if they ring we must ring them. We must do something to cause them to ring. Every life may hear their happy echoes, every life may be joyous. If our life does not hold a considerable content of joy it is because we permit it to become abnormal. We permit the joy bells to hang silent in the belfries of our souls.

Like all other capacities our capacity for joy and gladness may be developed and increased. It is important to have the will to be joyful. "I mean to be happy" should be the motto of each of us. There need be nothing selfish in such an attitude. It is perfectly right and in complete harmony with God's will that we hold such an attitude and that we use our best endeavors to make it a reality in our lives.

The Christian religion is not long-faced and gloomy. It is the greatest source of true happiness. We should set ourselves the task of developing our capacity to be happy. We should not be like a woman who once lived neighbor to my grandfather. She constantly wore a sunbonnet that extended some inches before her face. Asked why she did it she said she wore it lest she should see something to make her laugh. A part of her idea of being a Christian was refraining from laughter. Others, while not so extreme, think it a mark of spirituality to be grave and dignified and to shut out of life whatever would make it bright, cheerful, and happy.

Long ago I determined to be happy. I determined to be happy no matter what happened and no matter what condition I might be in or what my circumstances might be. For twenty-one years I have been bedfast, a constant sufferer, but I am happy. I am happy every day. I will not be any other way. I have had my troubles, many of them. I shall probably have more. I have learned that troubles do not make unhappiness. It is only a wrong attitude toward trouble that does so. I hope the reader will pardon my referring to my own experience, but I have passed through so much suffering and trouble and have learned to be happy in spite of it that I know others can do the same if they will. Many a time I have had to pull hard on the rope of the joy bells to get them to ring. I have kept on pulling until they pealed out their joyous tones. You can do the same no matter what the situation or surroundings, if you will go about it in the right way.

Many people have unfavorable tendencies. They seem naturally disposed to be easily discouraged or gloomy, to look on the dark side. They are timid, sensitive, or unsociable. These unfavorable natural tendencies should not be permitted to have sway.

We should set ourselves resolutely to overcome such tendencies. If we are inclined to become easily discouraged we should cultivate hope. We should ask ourselves, "What would be the hopeful attitude with regard to this situation?" Having determined what it would be we should adopt it and hold it no matter what the temptation is to do otherwise.

If we are inclined to be gloomy and to look on the dark side, let us compel ourselves to look on the bright side. Perhaps we may feel there is no bright side, but there is always a bright side to everything. If there is no naturally bright side let us turn it up toward God and let the sunshine of his love fall upon it. That will brighten any circumstance. If we are inclined to be timid let us compel ourselves to do what we ought to do or want to do. Let us not surrender to our timidity. We can break through it, overcome, it, master it. If we give way to it, its hold upon us becomes firmer and firmer. If we do what we desire to do in spite of it, it will cease to hinder us.

If we are inclined to be unsociable we should compel ourselves to act in a friendly way whether we feel like it or not. We should practice being friendly toward others. We should meet them halfway or beyond. If we act this out, friendliness will soon become natural to us and bring us much satisfaction.

I have spoken of the rope of the joy bells. Most bells do not ring of themselves. We must ring them. So we must ring the joy bells. Sometimes our joy bells seem like the old bell on a farm where I once was. It stood on a tall pole. I wondered why it was not rung to call the workers in from the field at noon. When I came to the house I discovered there was no rope attached to the bell.

In some cases the joy bells are like a bell on another farm where I lived. It did not hang in the proper position because it was not properly balanced. So when the wind would blow the bell would ring night or day. Many a time I was awakened in the night by its ringing. Some joy bells likewise ring only as chance occurrences. They ring only under favorable conditions, as a result of favorable circumstances. They are not controlled. We need to attach a rope of faith to our joy bells and through the exercise of this faith we can cause them to ring. We can have an inner source of joy and peace that is not disturbed by the storms of life, that does not depend upon circumstances, but has its root and fountain deep in the heart. We can be so hid away with Christ in God that the storms will pass us by.

A number of years ago during the test of a submarine it stayed submerged for many hours. When it returned to the harbor a man said to the commander, "Well, how did the storm affect you last night?" The commander looked at him in surprise and said, "Storm! We knew nothing of any storm!" They had been down far enough below the surface not to feel the storm. We can sink down into God from life's storms so they need not keep the joy bells of our souls from ringing. We can be joyful even in the midst of trouble.

A friend once told me of his experience in an earthquake. He said when the buildings trembled and swayed all the bells of the city began ringing. In life's earthquakes we may so trust God that our joy bells will ring.

God gives us the gift of joy. Jesus said he gives us his peace that our joy may be full. Paul rejoiced in the midst of his tribulations. "We are exceeding joyful in all our tribulation" [2 Cor. 7:4]. And he exhorted the Thessalonians to "rejoice evermore." If we cannot rejoice in the present realization of our hopes, we can at least rejoice in hope of better things to come. Rejoicing in past victories and in past blessings will often bring joy in spite of present trouble.

There may be dark periods in life. Failure may cast its shadows upon us. Discouragements may press us. If we look only at the present we shall have a hard time to make the joy bells ring. At such times we should look at our lives as a whole, not at these temporary incidents. "Weeping may endure for a night, but joy cometh in the morning" [Ps. 30:5]. Morning will dawn upon our darkest night. If we cannot rejoice in ourselves in the present we can rejoice in God. We can rejoice in the good things of the past and in the good things that lie before us in the future.

The truly and permanently happy people are those who have a source of happiness too deep or too high to be seriously disturbed by ordinary troubles. We can attain a stability that makes us like the anchored buoy rather than like a drifting object ever tossed about by the waves of circumstances. Faith is the anchor of the soul. In fact faith is the most essential element in a life of happiness and success. Those who have this inner source of happiness do not depend upon daily events to make them happy. They depend upon what they are, upon their relations with God; they live by faith settled, rooted, and grounded in Christ and in the Christian life. The waves of trouble may pass over them, but they are not swept from their place.

Jesus taught us a valuable lesson when he said, "I have meat that ye know not of" [John 4:32]. We may know what this means from personal experience. We may be so submitted to God, so obedient to him, and so trustful that the joy bells may be kept ringing and our souls be rejoicing evermore until we reach that land of endless day where trouble and sorrow, discouragements and suffering, never come. Learn how to ring your joy bells and how to prevent them from being muffled by doubts and fears.

39.

Just for Today

There are three days—yesterday, today, and tomorrow. Each person in the world lives in one of these three days. Some are living in the present, some in the past, and some in the future. Where we are living with respect to time has a great influence upon our lives. Perhaps we do not know just where we are living. It might pay us to make a careful examination and see whether the past, the present, or the future is bulking most largely in our thoughts and conversation.

Those who live in yesterday are living on memories. Yesterday is gone forever. We can never recall it. I once knew a home where the wife had died. I visited it a year or so after her death. It was a gloomy place. The husband was a gloomy man. He had tried to leave everything in the home as nearly as possible as his wife had left it. The musical instrument had been untouched. This man was living in the past. All his brightness, joy, love, and happiness were in the past. The present meant nothing to him. The future held no hope. On the journey of life he was walking backward. His gaze was ever behind him.

Many are like this man. Their circumstances may be different, but they are facing the past. Their only joys are the memory of past joys. Their sorrow over past troubles, mistreatments, losses, failures, and sins shrouds their lives in gloom. Why should we keep these memories ever present with us? Bring not the cares of the past, its regrets, sorrows, or anything from it that can cast a gloom upon our today, into the lives we are now living. Yesterday is only a memory. Let us carefully cover its scars. Let us not exhibit them to the world. Let us not be ever looking upon them and thinking over them. Paul's example is a good one to follow, "Forgetting that which is behind I press toward the mark" [Phil. 3:14]. We should let yesterday be yesterday. Someone has said,

"The tears of yesterday are like passing showers." After the shower should come sunshine. After yesterday's troubles should come forgetting. Yesterday's joys should be succeeded by the joys of today. Let us not live in yesterday. Today is too full of opportunity. It is heavily laden with good things. Let us dry the tears of yesterday. Let us turn to today.

Other people live in tomorrow. Their joys are the joys of anticipation, not of realization. True, anticipation has its real joys, but we should not picture a tomorrow so bright that it obscures today. We should not exalt tomorrow so much that today loses its meaning. The hopes of tomorrow, the bright pictures we paint, are not reality. We know not whether they ever will be. Sometimes people cannot enjoy today because of their forebodings for tomorrow. Instead of filling the future with bright anticipations, they fill it with a thousand ghostly fears. They cross their bridges before they get to them and because they are ever looking at the bridges which their imagination pictures before them they cannot see the beauties beside the roadway they are traveling.

For them the flowers bloom in vain. The songs of the birds are not heard. The beautiful prospects on each side of their way are lost. The bridge ahead is what they see. Their attention is so focused on it that they have no eyes or ears for today. A writer said, "I am the champion bridge crosser. I not only cross them but I help build them." He has many relatives today scattered all over the world. They are in the same business. The fears of tomorrow are a blight on many todays.

Jesus, who understood life better than anyone else, said, "Take therefore no thought for tomorrow, for the morrow shall take thought for the things of itself" [Matt. 6:34]. His meaning is—do not live in tomorrow, do not borrow trouble. Live tomorrow when you get to it. Live in today. We know not what tomorrow will bring forth. When it comes it will take thought for itself. There will be time enough to meet its problems, to overcome its difficulties, to fight its battles, and to rejoice in its victories when we have reached them. Let us not neglect today for tomorrow.

Whittier says,

> No longer forward or behind
> I look in hope or fear,
> But grateful take the good I find
> The best of now and here.

Our lives are wholly made of todays. Let us live in the time that is ours; make the best of it while we may. Let us enjoy its joys and do its work. Let us live to the full today, giving to the past and to the future only what is justly theirs and only what will profit us in the giving.

It is important that we properly meet things as they come. Someone has said, "Tomorrow we shall smile over today's worries; so why not begin today?" This is an excellent philosophy and well worth consideration. If adopted it will be a profitable rule of life.

If we were given now the strength and grace we shall need tomorrow we could not use it. It would profit us nothing. If we are strong enough for today, tomorrow need give us no concern. We shall be strong enough for it when it comes. Sufficient for today is God's way of giving. Suppose you try using today the strength and grace you had yesterday. Does it avail you anything? Then do not look for tomorrow's grace today, for if you had it today you could not use it either tomorrow or today.

We should not attempt to solve all the future's problems now or to see our way entirely clear before us. Face whatever is right at hand. Sometimes the difficulties of today have a way of projecting themselves into the future so that when we look forward we feel we never can bear what will be.

Perhaps a little more of my own experience may be helpful. When I was forced to remain bedfast my sufferings were very great. These continued month after month. The future loomed before me so dark, so discouraging, so hopeless, that I felt I never could face it. I asked myself, "How can I endure it?" I was appalled by the prospect. While I was in this melancholy state it seemed the Spirit of God drew near and whispered to me, "You do not have to live tomorrow now. You do not need to bear tomorrow's pain or suffering now. God knows what you can bear. He will not let more come upon you than you can bear. Live today, not the days that are before you."

I said within myself, "Yes, God knows what I can bear. He will not let that come which is too great for me. I will live today. I can bear this today. I will not think of tomorrow." And so again and again I said to myself, "I can bear it today." This attitude was a great help to me, and the sense of God watching over my life became much more real.

Yes, you can bear it today. Whatever your trouble, whatever your sorrow, whatever your perplexity, you will find a way of getting through today. When tomorrow comes there will be a way for tomorrow. Not long ago I was reading the hymn, "Lead, Kindly Light," and was deeply impressed by some of its ideas. The author says, "I do not ask to see, the distant scene, one step enough for me." He had come to live in today. But was this a natural characteristic? By no means. He continues, "I was not ever thus.... I loved to choose and see my path." How human he was. How like the rest of us! But he learned the wisdom of living in today, until he could say, "One step enough for me." In confidence he closes:

> So long Thy power hath blest me, sure it still
>   Will lead me on
> O'er moor and fen, o'er crag and torrent, till
>   The night is gone.

Today has enough for us to bear, enough for us to conquer, enough work for us to do. But we shall be sufficient for it. Many of our troubles of today will pass with today. We need not carry them into the future. We can meet our troubles of today as Abraham Lincoln met his. One biographer wrote, "Lincoln even when assailed by such anxieties and griefs as you never will know used to say, 'And this too will pass.'"

Yes, today will pass and tomorrow will come, and when tomorrow comes we shall have tomorrow's strength for its needs. Let us live today, in the strength that God gives, and not permit the shadows of yesterday or forebodings for tomorrow to hide the sunshine and beauty and gladness that come from trust and obedience today.

If You Can't Help It

We should like to have the ability to make things go as we wish them to go. We should like to accomplish everything we attempt. We desire all our plans to work out as we plan them. We should like to avoid all disappointments, all failures, all wrecking of our hopes and plans. Unfortunately, or perhaps sometimes fortunately, we cannot always accomplish what we desire. There are none of us who cannot look back upon mistakes, failures, and losses that bring us regret. I suppose all of us would like to change many things. We should like to have the opportunity of trying again.

Perhaps we realize that the failure was our own fault. Perhaps we look back upon errors, indiscretions, blunders, that humiliate and trouble us. We live under the shadow of them. Some of us are saying to ourselves, "Oh, if I had not done it. Oh, if I had done differently." Others are saying, "I failed. What is the use to try again?"

Others look back upon evils that came upon them seemingly through no fault of their own. They cannot get away from these influences, or at least they do not do so. A blight from the past withers all the present. What shall we do with the past? We cannot live over those days that are gone. We cannot have another chance wherein we failed. We cannot turn the clock of time back to yesterday. We are here in today. Those things are back in yesterday. We are eternally separated from them so far as having power to change them is concerned. We cannot help the past.

There is but one thing left for us—to make the best of the present. We cannot make the best of the present if we bring into it the past so that it becomes a present hindrance. Some wrongs of the past may be righted. Some evils may be undone. If so, instead of letting their shadows rest upon our lives and their weight upon our consciences we should make haste to do all that can be done to right them. There are people who should make right wrongs they have done to others. I shall not tell you to pass these by or to forget them. Instead I must say it is your duty to do everything possible to make right any wrongs of the past.

I am talking in this chapter of past deeds we cannot change, not of damage we can repair. There can be no excuse for not doing what we can do to repair errors of the past. At the same time many circumstances can never be improved by anything we may do. No effort of ours can make them better. We may regret them ever so much. We may be humiliated by them. The memory of them may be a constant trouble, goading us all the time. What shall we do about such things? I find in my notebook a stanza, the origin of which I do not know:

> For every evil under the sun
> There is a remedy or there is none;
> If there is one, try to find it;
> If there is none, never mind it.

This is excellent advice. If there is a remedy for the past try earnestly to find it, but what cannot be remedied should be left to the past. Shakespeare says, "What's gone, and what's past help, should be past grief." We should shut the door of the past lest the chilling breezes that blow through cause us to be unable to make proper use of the present. Paul had memories that troubled him. Mention is made here and there in his writings of his much regretted past. The blood of God's saints was upon his garments. He remembered the bitterness and hatred he had put into the pitiless persecution that he had visited upon the Christians. He remembered his part in the death of Stephen. He remembered how he had witnessed against many, had thrown many into prison, had brought many to death. He could not change the past. There was but one thing he could do. He resolved to do what was possible to do. He said, "One thing I do. Forgetting those things that are behind I press toward the mark."

Ah, yes, forgetting the past. We should like to forget, but, alas, we cannot forget. Neither could Paul forget in the sense of banishing the past from his memory. He could forget, however, in a very practical sense, and this he did. He did not let his past errors hinder him from living a life of freedom and activity, of love and sacrifice, of wholehearted devotion to the Christ he had hated. He threw all his energies into today. He did not let vain regrets hinder him. Perhaps those regrets, deep and poignant as they were, often pressed in upon him, but he pushed them aside and threw himself anew into the work he was doing, perhaps even more zealously than he would have done or could have done had he not been spurred on by these regrets.

Some are chained to the past by griefs and sorrows. Some live in the past with loved ones who have gone to a brighter clime. Some homes are kept darkened and the voice of music is hushed. A dead hand lies upon the heart and upon the home. Such a sorrow can be a blight on the

46.

life. What shall we do? Shall we tear affection from our hearts? Shall we put from us thoughts of the happy past? No, we need not do this, but we must not walk with our sorrow and commune with it until it becomes the greatest fact in our lives.

We must resolutely overcome blighting sorrow. We must live in today. There may be a sort of grim pleasure in living in a cemetery. Such a life is but a living death. Our loved ones would not wish us thus to sorrow for them. They would desire us to enter into the activities of today. They would be remembered but not with a sorrow so deep and absorbing that it shuts out any of the happiness that might come to us today or prevents us from filling the useful place we might fill.

There are others who are not so troubled about the yesterdays as they are about today. Certain people have within themselves qualities that are constantly getting them into trouble. They are of an unfortunate temperament, or they have certain characteristics that constantly hurt or antagonize others. They try to curb themselves, but often fail. To be sure we should resolutely endeavor to be masters of ourselves, but if we have qualities in our make-up that we cannot help, we cannot help them; that is all there is to it. We should do all we can, but when we have done all we can we should adjust ourselves to the facts. We should not permit these faults to blight our lives.

When the Lord accepted us he accepted us with those shortcomings in us. He knew all about them. If they did not prevent his accepting us they will not prevent his continuing to love us. They will not prevent our serving him acceptably. They may cause us trouble and humiliation, but if we cannot help it we cannot help it, so we must make the best of it.

Have you tried again and again to overcome some fault and still it troubles you? Well, Paul had such an experience. Of course you remember that oft-mentioned "thorn in the flesh" [2 Cor. 12:7]. Paul tried to get rid of that, but the Lord did not take it away. He said, "My grace is sufficient" [2 Cor. 12:9]. In other words, he said to Paul, "I am not going to take that away from you. I am going to leave it there to work a good purpose in you. I know what it will work out. You put up with it. You make the best of it. I will see that you come out all right." Now the Lord may talk that way to us or at least may hold that attitude toward us. Paul went ahead and made the best of an unpleasant situation. He succeeded. We may do likewise.

Sometimes we are tempted to look upon ourselves as failures. I suppose all of us came short of our hopes and expectations many times. One thing, however, is certain. We shall never be real failures unless we surrender to circumstances and give up the fight. Sometimes out of failure come the greatest victories. People who seem to be the greatest failures sometimes prove to be the greatest successes. A quotation concerning Abraham Lincoln has in it a lesson of perseverance under the most trying and disconcerting circumstances one can imagine. As you read, think if you have had more failures in your life than he or more cause to give up trying:

> When Abraham Lincoln was a young man he ran for the legislature in Illinois, and was badly swamped.
>
> He next entered business, failed, and spent seventeen years of his life paying up the debts of a worthless partner.
>
> He was in love with a beautiful young woman to whom he became engaged—then she died.
>
> Entering politics again he ran for Congress and was badly defeated. He then tried to get an appointment in the United States Land Office but failed.

He became a candidate for the United States Senate and was badly defeated.

In 1856 he became a candidate for the Vice-Presidency and was once more defeated.

In 1858 he was defeated by Douglas.

One failure after another—bad failures—great setbacks. In the face of all this he eventually became one of the greatest men of America, his memory loved and honored throughout the world.

These do not exhaust the catalogue of Lincoln's failures. Many others might be added to this list. But was Lincoln a failure? By no means. Neither need you be, notwithstanding all the failures you make.

Perhaps the greatest "failure" the world ever saw was Jesus of Nazareth. Seeking to do a great work, he came to his own, but his own rejected him. They hardened their hearts against him. They opposed him most bitterly. Again and again he had to escape for his life, and at last he was taken, condemned, ignominiously crucified. He who had proclaimed himself Son of God was now a pauper, laid in a borrowed tomb, leaving his disciples disappointed, chagrined, hopeless, despairing. But was that the end? Ah, no, he rose again to be the world's Redeemer.

The question is not, Have we made failures? or, Shall we make other failures? We shall never become blunder-proof. We shall not always be wise and discreet in our conduct. We do not know enough always to avoid such errors. Then, too, we are often taken by surprise and have to act without consideration. Of course, we shall not always do the wisest and best thing.

We also have weaknesses, and these weaknesses will sometimes assert themselves. Perfection in the realm of human conduct is not of this world. Paul speaks of that which is perfect as being in the future. When that comes we shall know as we are known. We shall see clearly, and we shall be wise and strong enough to meet, as they should be met, all the circumstances that arise. But now we are imperfect. We have our weaknesses and short-comings. We should not surrender to them. We should not allow them to blight our lives, discourage us, or make us feel that we are failures. We should resolutely make the best of them and face life with courage. But do you say, "I am so ashamed of my blunders and weaknesses"? Wesley's advice to his fellow ministers was, "Never be ashamed of anything but sin."

If you cannot be what you desire to be, be what you can be and do not be ashamed of it. Do not let mistakes or imperfections prevent you from doing what you should do. I remember one young man who succeeded in getting a position that paid him a salary which for that day was looked upon as being rather unusual. Through a combination of circumstances he lost that position. It was not his fault. His conduct reflected honor upon him. He sacrificed greatly to do what he did. He felt he was wronged. He returned to his home, surrendered to circumstances, gave up to discouragements, and so far as I have learned permitted his life to be ruined.

This is an example of what we should avoid. But are you doing the same thing? Are you following out the same principle? If so, cease to do so. Be the man or the woman you can be. Hold up your head, look circumstances in the face, and say, "I have failed, but I am not a failure. I have failed, but I will yet succeed."

People have to face many misfortunes—home troubles, business reverses, debts, physical handicaps. Look upon the great names of history and see how many of them had such things to meet, but in spite of them went resolutely forward.

Many people seem to do well until some crisis comes and they fail. This failure seems to change the whole course of their lives. They look upon their lives differently and hold a different attitude toward themselves than formerly. I had such an experience. Actively engaged in evangelistic work, feeling that I was prepared to do more effectual work than hitherto, having plenty of opportunities for work, I was hopeful, even confident of success. In the midst of this I was stricken. Worst of all I realized that I had brought it upon myself. Lying upon my bed, suffering day and night without respite, I would look back to the time I was injured and think I had no one to blame but myself. That it was an accident wholly unexpected, that I had no way of foreseeing it and so could not have avoided it, did not change the fact. I had brought it upon myself. Oh, the days and months of self-condemnation, of bitter regret! It darkened all nature. It brought me to the verge of despair.

Again and again I said to myself, "I am only a has-been. The future holds nothing desirable. I have nothing to look forward to. So far as my work is concerned and my life among men I had better be dead." For eight long weary years no ray of hope shone for the future. But I learned to make the best of the present, to turn resolutely away from the past and to cease self-condemnation. After I had learned this lesson God opened the door of opportunity to me again in a most unexpected way. He has given me larger opportunity than ever before, and to the glory of his grace I believe he has made me more useful than I ever should have been without learning these hard lessons.

Whatever there may be in your life that cannot be helped, do not sit down and fold your hands and spend your days mourning. Make the best of it. There is a way out, and that way leads to victory and success.

Ingrowing Thoughts

A woman said of a certain person who frequently had trouble in her spiritual life, "Her chief trouble is that her thoughts turn inward too much." Ingrowing thoughts, like ingrowing toenails, are sometimes very painful. There is such a thing as focusing our thoughts too much inwardly. Wherever we center our thoughts we produce a reaction. Centering our thoughts on our own spiritual difficulties, on our own inner experiences, and upon our feelings and sensations is likely to produce an effect entirely different from what we desire.

Dr. Stephen Smith, hale, hearty, and happy at the age of ninety-nine, said among other things in stating his philosophy of life, "War has killed its millions, but introspection has killed its tens of millions. Next to an ill-advised and overplentiful diet it has shortened more lives than almost any other cause that we can name. The man who is forever thinking about himself is degenerating. The hardest patients I have had to handle were those given to introspection and self-analysis."

Note those persons who are extremely careful about themselves in physical matters. They are always concerned with what effect food and weather and the rest will have upon them. They wonder if this will hurt them and how that will affect them. They are afraid of taking cold, and of this, that, and the other thing. They make living too serious a business. They are nearly always the victims of their own carefulness. The one who gets along well physically is usually the one who uses good common sense and then practically forgets he has a body.

In spiritual things it is the people who are always taking their spiritual temperature, and looking at their spiritual tongue, and feeling their spiritual pulse, and measuring their spiritual stature, who have the most trouble. Some people are always questioning their own motives. They are constantly asking, "Should I have done that?" They give microscopic attention to the details of their life. They are all the time asking, "Did I do right? Am I right?" Everything must be minutely examined. The smallest detail of life must not be passed without attention.

It is true that the Bible says, "Examine yourselves" [2 Cor. 13:5], but it has no reference to such microscopic examinations. If we should be going somewhere and our foot should slip we would not take for granted that we had turned around and headed in the opposite direction. That one little slip is but an incident in the journey. When the path is observed as a whole that little incident is only a trifle. The general course has been forward.

Some people cannot sing the song of Christian joyfulness because they are too much absorbed in examining themselves. Neither do they feel like singing, for they are constantly finding little faults and magnifying them out of all proportion to their significance. We all know people who have ingrowing thoughts. It is proper for us to pay due heed to ourselves, but this ought to occupy a comparatively small portion of our time. Some people have so much trouble keeping themselves right that they never get anything else done. The trouble is they are making too hard a task of it. They would be just as nearly right without making half, or perhaps a tenth, of the effort. In other words, if they did not make such an effort they would not even then go wrong. We need rather to be concerned to have sufficient velocity to produce a momentum that will keep us on the way. When I first started to learn bicycle riding it took all my attention to keep balanced, and in spite of myself I would fall over now and then. I soon became enough accustomed to riding that I guided the wheel automatically and gave no more attention to balance than when walking. At first I was constantly turning the wheel this way and that. Consequently I made a crooked path. That is why many

Christians do so poorly. They are so intent upon keeping themselves right that they have their eyes constantly upon themselves. Let them look ahead, become intent on reaching what lies before them, and they will make real progress. They will not fall over nearly so easily as when they are so careful about themselves.

In studying ourselves and losing sight of others we become morbid. We brood over our shortcomings or seeming shortcomings. We lose our courage. Life looks dark and discouraging. We may say that Satan is after us, that he is accusing us. Most accusations have their origin in ourselves. We are accusing ourselves. We are condemning ourselves and imagine that it is Satan doing so.

We ought to understand that our minds have two arts. Much goes on in our minds of which we are conscious. We think certain thoughts and know we think them. We consciously follow out certain ideas. On the other hand, there is a part of our mind of whose workings we are unaware. This is called the subconscious.

You have often noticed that a plan all worked out and complete comes into your mind apparently from nowhere. Or you are suddenly affected by an motion. You cannot account for feeling that emotion. If it is a pleasant emotion, you enjoy it and think little about it. If it is an unpleasant one, you nay be troubled by it and wonder what caused it. The secret of the matter is that much has been going on in your subconscious mind of which you new nothing. Suddenly what was in your subconscious was projected into your conscious mind.

Perhaps a few days ago you wondered over something that happened and questioned whether or not you were what you ought to be spiritually. That thought presently faded out of your mind. You thought no more about it. A week, two weeks, or a month later, you suddenly, and without any seeming reason, felt a sense of condemnation come over you. You wondered what caused it. Perhaps you thought Satan was at work. You did not understand that the thought you had the other day and and forgotten about kept on working in your subconscious mind and just now projected itself into your conscious mind.

This is the secret of much of our trouble. Those accusations you had did not come from Satan. They are the product of your own thoughts. You started the thought working, then got your mind off on something else. But that did not get the thought out of your mind. What shall we do to hinder such thoughts from working in our mind and having such a depressing, discouraging effect upon us? When the idea that starts this train of thought comes into your mind, meet it with an assertion of faith in God's promises. Drive the idea from your mind with some good thought. Assure your heart that God is with you and is taking care of you and that you can meet whatever comes. This will uproot the other thought from your mind, and it will not continue to work in your subconscious mind.

Remember, when you allow yourself to think discouraging thoughts, when you allow yourself to question your motives and examine yourself with such attentive scrutiny, you are loading up your subconscious mind with what sooner or later will come out into your conscious mind again to trouble you. Therefore, do not plant such seeds of troublesome thoughts in your mind. Plant thoughts of faith, of victory, of trust, of assurance, of confidence, and these will bear fruit that you will be glad to reap.

We can imagine untruths about ourselves as easily as we can imagine them about others. Our imagination can be misdirected. C. B. Larson has said, "Imagination when misdirected can produce more ills than any other faculty." Many people are tortured by their imagination. Imaginary ills and imaginary foes beset them.

Of course we shall have heartaches. Of course we shall have experiences we can hardly keep from thinking over.

But we should avoid magnifying them. We should treat them with good common sense. Instead of lavishing so much time upon ourselves and trying so hard to keep ourselves right, if we turn our attention toward helping others, we find many of our own troubles cured without any medicine. About two-thirds of our troubles might be cured by forgetting them.

If you were busy being glad,
And cheering others who were sad,
Altho' your heart might ache a bit,
You'd soon forget to notice it.

Most of our troubles are imaginary or at least nine-tenths imaginary. Paul speaks about "casting down imaginations" (2 Cor. 10:5). That is something we should all learn. Do not expect of yourself more than you expect of others. Judge yourself by the same standards by which you judge others. God does not want you to be melancholy. He wants you to be joyful, to sing the songs of his kingdom, to have a heart full of praises. To have these you must turn your eyes to God often and see his beauties and perfections. Forget yourself and think of God and his goodness.

The fruits of thoughts are feelings. If you do not think right you cannot feel right. Naturally when you do not feel as you think you ought to feel, you are ready to condemn yourself and say, "Well, there must be something wrong." Yes, there is something wrong, but in the majority of instances that wrong is merely in your thoughts. If there is something actually wrong in your heart, wrong in your relations with God, or wrong in your relations with your fellow men, you can locate that easily. It is something definite. It is not something that you need seek for days and cannot find. The things that stand between us and God, or between us and others, if they are worth noticing at all, are at least large enough to be easily discovered and are definite enough to be easily understood. The remedy for them is easily applied and its results are definite and easily known.

We should understand clearly that those obscure misgivings, the cause of which we cannot locate, though they bring gloom, despondency, and discouragement, originate in a wrong outlook or in a wrong attitude toward ourselves. They are the fruits of wrong thinking.

So let us get rid of our ingrowing thoughts. Let us get outside of ourselves into the sunshine of God. Then our hearts will become light. We shall see the goodness of God, and almost before we know it we shall be singing the song of the victorious life.

Troublesome Neighbors

Sometimes an otherwise pleasant neighborhood can be kept in an uproar by a few troublemakers. Human troublemakers, however, are not to be compared with some other kinds.

I am fortunate enough to have splendid neighbors. Nevertheless, even in this good neighborhood ere is a great deal of trouble. The names of the troublemakers are not Jones and Adams and Thompson, or anything of that sort. There are three of these families of troublemakers. Two of them are the "ifs" and the "maybes." Not far away are the "buts," who are close relatives of the others. Most of these belong to the "doubt" family or their close neighbors, the "unwillings."

"These "ifs" and "buts" are a numerous brood. They are quite vocal. They are always ready to make suggestions. They are full of questions. They are constantly reminding us of the uncertainty of life, and not infrequently they make it appear much more uncertain than it really is.

Let me introduce some of the "ifs." Here is one, "If I were just sure." This one suggests that you don't really know. You should be a little more certain. You might make a mistake. Perhaps you are already acquainted with this fellow. He says, "If I were just sure I am saved"; "If I were just sure I am right"; "If I could know so that I could not question it."

How many times you have been tormented by this bad neighbor! Perhaps you were satisfied for a time about your experience, or about other things, but then you fell to questioning and wondering. This "if" makes you frequent visits, but is never a welcome guest. You have to deal with him some way. Are you able to do so satisfactorily?

Another "if" says, "If I didn't feel so..." Yes, you would like to have pleasant feelings all the time, but that cannot always be. Whenever you have feelings you dislike, or that cause you trouble, this "if" is ready to suggest that you should not be too sure of your position. He says you should not undertake any spiritual work until you feel certain. You agree with him and say, "If I didn't feel so..."

A full brother to this "if" is, "If things didn't seem so..." To be sure, life sometimes seems awry. People and things are not as they ought to be. We cannot get conditions to seem right. We are troubled, restless, and uncertain because of the trouble this "if" gives us.

The next "ifs" are twins. "If I were not tempted so," and "If I were not tried so." Yes, how happy you could be if it were not for these twins. But they are your close neighbors. They visit you every now and then. And how tormenting they can be! If you could move away and leave them you would rejoice. But if you should move they would move with you. You must always expect to have them as neighbors, so you must find a way of adjusting yourself to them, so that they will not spoil your happiness or hinder your Christian growth.

Another "if" that has brought terror to many a soul is, "If I am not right." This "if" can visit you on nearly any occasion. It has no manners. It may come in the dead of night. It may come when you are getting along well. It may come when you are having troubles, when you are bothered, tempted, or not feeling well physically. But whenever it comes it tends to give you a spiritual shock. It makes you ask the question, "What if I am mistaken?" or sometimes, "What if I am deceived?" A great many people suffer because they fear to be deceived. It is needless to suffer from such fear. God will not let an honest soul be deceived with respect to its relations with him. It is only the ones who will not have the truth to whom he sends delusions. It is our privilege to know our situation and not to worry about being deceived. Sin is deceitful, but righteousness, never.

Another "if" of the "doubt" family is, "If God doesn't…" We must have help from God. We put our trust in him. But what if he should fail us? What if his promises should not be fulfilled?

Another "if" is "If I fail." The possibility of failure is ever before us and we can let this "if" be a great barrier to all our efforts if we will. These are only a few of the "ifs" that live close neighbors to many of us.

We now turn our attention to the "but" family. First, "But I" says, "But I am so weak." Then it shows all our weakness. It calls our attention to the failures of the past. It pictures how likely we are to fail in the future. Yes, we should like to do this, that, or the other, but "my weakness!" It also says, "But my ignorance. If I try, I shall only blunder."

In psychological circles much is said about inferiority complexes. A great many people have a sense of inferiority. They think others can do better than they, that others are better than they are. They think they must always be in the rear of the procession. They are always minimizing their own abilities and their various good qualities. "But" is the favorite word of this inferiority complex. It can always imagine difficulties that do not exist.

Another of this family is, "But they." It is the expression of man fear. "But they will say"; "But they will think"; "But they will do." Many people are held back and their lives stunted by constant fear of what others think, say, or do.

These "buts" and "ifs" and all their kind have one spokesman who says the final word. When it is pointed out to us that there are ways to overcome all these troublesome neighbors, when we are exhorted to be free, to be our real selves, to rise above our fears, when our friends would instill courage into us, then this spokesman is heard. "Yes, but maybe," he says. He admits all that has been said, but still has additional fears to bring up.

What will you do with these "buts," these "ifs," these troublesome neighbors of yours? You have to do something with them. Sometimes you can ignore them. At other times you have to use other methods to overcome them. Anyway, you must overcome them before you will have learned the secret of the singing heart. As long as you are tormented by these you will not feel like singing. It is possible for you to look all these "ifs" and "buts" in the face and then go unfalteringly on your way heavenward.

You must put them to rout with the sword of faith. You must shield yourself from their darts with the shield of faith. The "ifs" and "buts" give faith its opportunity. Faith is intended as an antidote for uncertainty and fear. It will cure the worst case of it. It will put to flight all your foes. It will silence your questioning. It will soothe your fears and quiet your troubled heart. It will make you conscious of your strength. It will enable you to overcome your temptations. It will keep you steadfast through your trials. It will enable you to trust regardless of your feelings. It will give you assurance.

A little girl, learning to punctuate, came home from school and told her mother what she had learned. Her mother said, "Indeed, and how did you do it?" "Well, Mama, it is just as easy as can be. If you say a thing is so, you just put a hatpin after it. But if you are only asking whether it is so or not, you put a buttonhook."

I fear some of us have too great a supply of buttonhooks. We are putting them after too many things. We need a greater supply of hatpins. Whenever God says anything, whenever he makes us a promise, be sure you put a hatpin after it. Your feelings will often tell you to use the buttonhook, but it does not belong there. It belongs after nothing that God says. So when you go to read your Bible, get a handful of hatpins. After every promise you read, put a hatpin. After everything God says, put a hatpin. Then be sure that later you do not replace it with a buttonhook.

Then, too, we need to put many hatpins after things in our own life. Say, "God will not fail," then put a hatpin after it. Say, "I shall not fail," and the hatpin. Settle things, then put hatpins after them and never allow yourself to change to buttonhooks. God wants us to be certain.

Faith is not only the antidote for fear and uncertainty. It is also the preventive of doubt and fear. Faith is the anchor of the soul. Anchor yourself with it by definitely exercising it each day.

In your life, do what God wants you to do. Do what duty demands, then make God responsible for the contingencies. When you work for anyone you obey his instructions, and then you let him be responsible for the consequences. That is exactly the way to do with God. Do his will, do your duty, and then do not be fearful of the consequences. Put the "ifs" and "buts" to rout. Keep up your shield of faith, wield your sword of faith, and you will conquer these enemies.

Erasing the Interrogation Marks

Life is full of mysteries. Many of them we wish we might understand. It would be much easier to go happily upon life's way if we could understand everything that happens to us, and if we could see our way before us.

We all ask questions. We all wonder why some things occur and what they mean. But some of us are more given to asking questions than others. Some put a question mark after everything. We have pointed out in the previous chapter some of the questions commonly asked. Many people form the habit of being uncertain. They cultivate indecision until it is difficult for them to make up their minds. Following this habit year after year increases the uncertainty of their lives. They are never quite sure.

How can we overcome uncertainty? First, we must set ourselves to the task of breaking ourselves of the habit of doubt. That is not easy, but it is possible. We should form right habits of thinking. We should not look upon people and circumstances and everything about us, as enemies. We should not live in a defensive attitude. We should not believe that everything we attempt to do will turn out bad, nor that everything is against us.

Most of life is in our favor. God created our environment, speaking in a general way, and he did not make that environment always hostile. It is true that there are many obstacles, many unfavorable influences. But the helpful ones are more numerous. The influences for good are more prevalent than are the evil ones. This is true when we hold the right attitude ourselves. God wants us to get the interrogation marks out of our relationships. He wants us to know definitely our relation to himself. He wants us to have an inner consciousness that our attitudes are acceptable to him. He wants us to have a religious experience with such basis of certainty that it brings us a constant assurance of rightness.

We need a consciousness of God's fatherhood. Many know from an intellectual standpoint that God is their Father, but they cannot realize it. They hope he is their Father. In a way they believe he is their Father, but when it comes to having the inner satisfaction of realizing the relation of sonship to him they know little of him. To them it is not a practical relation.

Some imagine God is ready to cut them off from him-self for any little trifling deviation from propriety. Their life is influenced more by fear of God than by love of God. If they are conscious of something worthy of reproof they count themselves estranged from God. Their joy is gone. Their attitude toward themselves and toward their relation to God is well illustrated by something a woman said to me recently, "If I had to ask the Lord to forgive me, I would think I had to get justified and sanc-tified over again."

Is God really our Father? Would he readily break those tender ties between his soul and ours and cast us into outer darkness because we had been overcome by some sudden temptation? Most of us have experienced God's disapproval. We recognized that we were in fault. As soon as the thing was done or said we immediately felt a pang of regret. Such errors may make a breach between us and God, but this breach is only partial and may at once be repaired.

If we take the right course God is ready to forgive. He is ready to repair the breach, to restore the interrupted fellowship. Experiences such as this are not interrup-tions of the Christian life; they are merely regrettable incidents in it. God cuts off only those who turn against him, who in spirit rebel against him.

Sin lies in the attitude of the will toward God. Many times our actions need repentance of a certain sort, but because the will has not turned away from God, they do not result in our being cut off from God. Perhaps we have all heard teaching that made a person either a Christian of angelic character and deportment or else a sinner rejected of God. Between these two lies a great middle ground. None of us are too angelic, but at the same time we are not servants of the devil. Between these two extremes lies a great range of human experience in which men walk with God, their heavenly Father, guided by his justice, but overshadowed with his mercy.

Often we think some strange thing has happened to us. We have experiences we cannot understand. Perhaps many of us have not learned God's method of dealing with his sons and daughters sufficiently to understand that what we feel is not his displeasure but his hand of discipline. He loves us with an everlasting love. That is not a love that can be easily broken. God's acts flow out of his love toward us. His everlasting love manifests itself in everlasting kindness. "I have loved thee with an everlasting love: therefore with lovingkindness have I drawn thee" (Jer. 31:3).

This is God's attitude toward all his children, even those who have faults and shortcomings. God does not expect us to be as wise as he is, or to exhibit the same power, or to be always as perfect as he is in our conduct. He does expect us to do right. He does expect us sincerely to try to please him. But he does not expect us to be free from blunders, mistakes, weaknesses, and those frailties that are commonly found in humanity. We should not excuse ourselves in doing anything improper. If we do so He will not excuse us. But with loving mercy he draws us back to him. As it is written, "As a father pitieth his children so the Lord pitieth them that fear him" [Ps. 103:13]. That pity manifests itself in his long-suffering, his tender mercy, his ready forgiveness.

One thing very difficult for many people to learn is that the chastening rod of God is applied in love, not in anger. We are told that God "scourgeth every son whom he receiveth" [Heb. 12:6] and that that scourging is the proof of our sonship. So often people are inclined to take it as evidence that they are no longer sons. They look upon it as a mark of God's disapproval or even of his anger. We are told that his chastening is for our profit. He does it not for his own pleasure, but that we may be made better by it. It is a mark of his love. He says, "As many as I love, I rebuke and chasten" (Rev. 3:19).

Read Hebrews 12:5–13. Note carefully God's attitude in his chastening. We are all ready to admit the truth of the eleventh verse, "No chastening for the present seemeth to be joyous, but grievous" [v. 11]. None of us like to be chastened, but yet that is necessary; out of it come the fruits of righteousness. When the Lord chastens us, therefore, let us bear it with meekness. Let us profit by it. Let us not be grieved and discouraged. The Lord says, "Wherefore lift up the hands which hang down, and the feeble knees" (v. 12). You can understand what that means. It means—stand up like a man. Do not bow down and tremble for fear. And he adds, "Make straight paths for your feet."

Gold is purified in the furnace. It is not destroyed; it is made the better by the flames. You and I must pass through the furnace. The purpose of the furnace is that we may be purged from our dross, that we may be refined, that we may be rid of grossness, that we may be made more spiritual. Does the gold ask, "Why hast thou put me into the furnace?" If you and I have to pass through the furnace of affliction or sorrow, of losses or failures, let us submit ourselves to the hand of God. Let us not question his mercy or his goodness; neither let us question ourselves. Let us endure as "seeing him who is invisible" [Heb. 11:27]. Let us trust his hand and his love. Let us not fear that we shall be destroyed.

We must often endure the chisel of pain as God carves in us his image. We desire to be in his image. We desire to be godly in character. Remember that God hurts only to heal. Like the surgeon he does not hurt willingly, but only of necessity. We have read of the balm a Gilead, but of what use is that balm until we are hurt? There would be no such balm were there no hurts in life.

God knows there are things that will hurt us. He knows that sufferings of various sorts are inevitable. He knows that we shall bring upon ourselves, by lack of wisdom or carefulness or understanding or in other ways, many humiliations and difficulties hard to endure. But He would not have these things unduly trouble us or make us feel that he has become our enemy. He would have us ever to recognize that he is our tender, compassionate Father. He would comfort us in our troubles as a mother comforts her children. In our times of trouble he would not have us run from him or shrink from his presence. He would have us run into his arms and tell him all our troubles, our questionings, our heartaches. He would have us so to trust him that the interrogation marks would be removed.

Many Christians are always on the defensive. They are always facing an enemy either without or within. Their lives are a constant battle with themselves, a struggle to repress something. They are constantly harassed lest they do wrong or feel wrong, lest they be deceived. They are a prey to apprehensions. They are constantly trying to strengthen themselves in an attitude of resistance against something. They hold themselves under a strain. They are constantly troubled over things that God would not have them be troubled over. Instead of living thus God wants us to live positively, to be on the offensive, to be victorious. He desires us to be courageous, confident, serene, and without anxiety, conscious of divine help.

Our openhearted God is a fountain of power. He would have our hearts open to receive his power. He would not have us trust in self but in his sufficiency of grace and power for every need. He would have us constantly believe that in any situation that may arise there will be no lack of what is necessary to make us overcomers. By believing this, and acting as though we believe it, we will be overcomers. We will rid ourselves of many of life's question marks. Some of them will remain to eternity, but many of them need trouble us no longer. Those that cannot be removed need not darken our lives. Trusting him we can go onward, singing the glad song that flows from the sense of his fatherhood and understanding love.

Building Blocks of Faith

Faith is one of the most powerful elements in human life. The eleventh chapter of Hebrews is a picture gallery of the heroes of faith. It begins with a definition of faith. We always need a definition that we may know what we are talking about. "Now faith is the substance ("ground or confidence," margin) of things hoped for, the evidence of things not seen" [Heb. 11:1]. The American Standard Version renders it thus, "Now faith is assurance of things hoped for, a conviction of things not seen." In the margin it reads, "Now faith is the giving substance to things hoped for, a test of things not seen."

This is a practical explanation rather than a definition of faith. Faith is accepting a promise or statement as true and acting upon it as truth, with all confidence. As it relates to God, it is taking God at his word. It is believing his promises. It is personal acceptance of his promises, relying on those promises, and making them the basis of life.

One phase of faith is confident trust; the other is confident action. We read of the "full assurance of faith." Such full assurance in the old-time worthies resulted in great accomplishments. In Hebrews 11 and elsewhere we read of what was done through faith. We look upon those who accomplished such things as, in some ways, superhuman. We are inclined to believe, as the doubters of this world believe, that the day of religious faith has largely passed. In reality that is not true. Mighty works of faith are being accomplished today. Faith is just as effective now as in any former age. People today have faith, and the power of their faith is manifested in mighty deeds and accomplishments.

We overlook the fact that when the worthies of Hebrews 11 were living, the people did not consider their faith as amounting to very much. They were probably entirely unaware of the great accomplishments of faith that were going on around them. In like manner, most people are ignorant of the wonderful accomplishments of faith that are so prevalent today.

When we read of the accomplishments of faith recorded in Hebrews 11 it is natural for us to say, "I am not like those men. I cannot have faith such as they had." I am not so sure of that. They were only common people with perhaps little more than average faith. It may be that we shall not accomplish all that they accomplished, but faith in us will produce real results just the same.

The day in which they lived was no more favorable for faith than today is. In fact there was not so much faith then as today. Christian knowledge and Christian experience have laid a broader ground for faith, a surer foundation than people had in former ages. Faith is just as mighty today and will accomplish as much as in ancient days. Perhaps we shall not duplicate the deeds they did. That may not be necessary; or perhaps it would not serve any good purpose if we should do so. But faith is the gift of God and he is willing to impart it to each of us.

We already have much natural faith. The faith we have is the basis of our lives. Without faith the business world could not operate. Home life would not be possible. Religion could not exist. Government would be powerless. No great undertakings would ever be begun. Accomplishments, of whatsoever sort, are based on faith.

No wonder we are urged in the Scriptures to "have faith in God."

Faith in God is believing him. We can have no satisfactory relations with him, except through faith. We are saved by faith. We are kept by faith. We are justified by faith. We stand by faith. We rejoice by faith. Assurance of immortality is a matter of faith. Faith is the victory that overcomes the world.

The apostles had faith. Jesus said to them, "Ye believe in God" [John 14:1]. Faith brings certainty. Without faith there can be no certainty. It brought certainty to Paul. He said, "I know whom I have believed, and am persuaded that he is able to keep that which I have committed unto him against that day" [2 Tim. 1:12].

God is worthy to be believed. He cannot lie because his whole nature is truth and righteousness. He never changes. He never forgets his promises. He never turns away from those who trust him. Therefore, have faith in God. We should hold the attitude toward the Word of God that was held by an old saint who was nearing the sunset of life. A minister quoted to her, "Lo, I am with you alway," and said, "What a blessed promise that is!"

"Ah," said she, "that is not a promise; that is just a fact."

God's promises are facts. They are actual facts or potential facts. They are either facts to us or may become facts to us by our trusting them. The greatest fact in the lives of God's people is that they believe God and they act upon that belief in a way that produces definite results in Christian living—holiness of heart and life, and true happiness. In fact, there can be no other basis for true happiness save faith. It is the foundation of all. To believe in God as the New Testament pictures him, to accept him as he is represented to be, and to submit to him as such faith would lead us to do, is to be happy.

One needful thing is that we believe in God as he reveals himself to be. We must do this quite apart from any inner feelings or fears we may have about him. He is what he reveals himself to be. If we feel he may be other than what he represents himself to be it is because we do not definitely believe the representation he makes of himself. We read God's promises, and often we cannot feel that they mean just what they say or that God will make them true to us. We fear and tremble when facing a crisis, though God has promised to be with us and help us. He has promised us victory through Jesus Christ all along the Christian way. Yet how many times we shrink and tremble and walk in uncertainty.

Unbelief is the source of all this weakness. Abraham believed God; therefore he did not stumble at God's promise. He took God at his word, then acted upon his word just as though there could be no such thing as questioning it. God's word is true. His promises were meant to be fulfilled. They are "yea and amen" to everyone who believes [2 Cor. 1:20]. God has no desire to avoid fulfilling that which he has promised to do. He is under no compulsion. He promised because he wanted to do the things he promised to do.

God will do what he has promised. Do you believe it? It is true, whether or not you believe it, but you will get the benefit of it only by believing it. You can believe it. You have the power to believe it. All fears that God will not do what he has promised are foolish fears. If you will believe, God will do the rest. If you will trust there will be no failure. If you will go ahead in faith, doubting nothing, your way will be prepared before you. The victory will ever be yours. You will be able to stand in the evil day. Whatever comes cannot overwhelm you. Your strength will be equal to your need. "Have faith in God" [Mark 11:22].

The psalmist declared that he would not fear though war was made upon him [Ps. 27:3]. That was the language of faith. Faith gave him courage. It will give you courage. There is no telling what God will do for those who trust him. What will earthly governments do for their citizens? Here is an illustration: Great Britain sent ten thousand men on a long voyage by sea, then seven hundred miles over sun-scorched trails through the jungles of Africa to fight their way through an armed and brave enemy to rescue one man. That man had been arrested and imprisoned illegally and unjustly. His life was at stake. So Great Britain risked the lives of ten thousand men that he might be saved.

If an earthly government will do this to save one of its citizens, what will the government of heaven do to save one of its citizens who appeals to it? Jesus said twelve legions of angels were ready to assist and defend him, and we are told that "the angel of the Lord encampeth round about them that fear him, to deliver them" [Ps. 34:7]. "Have faith in God."

The life of faith is the most satisfactory of all lives. In fact it is the only satisfactory life. Matthew Henry wrote, "None live so easily, so pleasantly, as those who live by faith."

Children implicitly trust their parents. They believe they will be protected and cared for. They believe their needs will be supplied. They believe they have nothing to fear. They have the confidence expressed by the little boy who was threatened with injury by a larger boy. He said as he looked the other squarely in the face, "No, you won't hurt me. My daddy won't let you." If we have the same confident trust in God we can say, "God will not let you" do the things that are threatened. God will protect us. God will help us.

This is not imagination. It is reality. We should cultivate an attitude of faith toward God, and expectancy that he will take care of us. This brings to us the confident assurance that we have nothing to fear. This in turn brings rest and peace. When we have learned to exercise such faith we have learned the secret of the singing heart.

C. B. Larson says, "We should train ourselves to meet everything in that attitude of mind that expects all things to work out right." Why should we not have such an attitude? Why should we not expect such results? We have every reason to be confident. Instead of questioning, fearing, trembling, lest we may fail, let us exercise definite faith in God, and day by day build up ourselves and erect a structure of Christian character and Christian life worthy of the God who helps us. Someone has said, "Do not wonder whether you will fail, but think how you are going to succeed." That is the attitude with which we should face life. Success is the product of faith. We should expect to succeed as well as determine to succeed.

Faith produces the building blocks wherewith we build up life. These building blocks of faith are not like the child's blocks with which it builds a tottery structure which falls at a touch. No, faith furnishes concrete blocks to build an enduring structure. With them we can build a life that the earthquakes of unfavorable circumstances cannot throw down.

Faith manifests itself in, or leads to, obedience. If we believe God is King and has the right to rule over us, and if we believe the Bible is his law, we will adopt an attitude of obedience. It will be our joy to do his will. Such faith will end rebellion. There will be no questioning, but sincere, wholehearted obedience. It will not be the obedience of fear but the obedience of love. Its language is, "I delight to do thy will, O God" [Ps. 40:8].

Faith also manifests itself in submission to God. God's will becomes sweet to us, and this submission to him becomes a great building force in our lives.

Faith results in honoring God by giving credit to his promises. If we "set to our seal that God is true" [cf. John 3:33], then we can say like the prophet, "They that be with us are more than they that be with them" (2 Kings 6:16). Faith has an inborn courage that can face any-

72.

thing. This courage is not the result of presumption. It is founded on solid facts.

It is not enough to believe in God. We must believe in ourselves as well. Oliver Wendell Holmes said, "Men who succeed have faith in themselves and faith in their fellows. Doubt either and you are doomed."

Sometimes it is easier to believe in God than to believe in ourselves, but there are abundant reasons why we should have faith in ourselves. If we know we are sincerely and earnestly trying to do God's will, if we know our purposes are right purposes and our actions are based on such purposes, we have an excellent foundation for faith in ourselves. I do not mean faith in ourselves apart from God, but faith that God and we are partners, that God and we can accomplish what is necessary to accomplish. God does not want us to go through life like shrinking criminals. He wants us to walk out boldly on the highways of life, unafraid that he will fail us and unafraid that we shall fail. We need self-respect. We need to have confidence in ourselves, in the sincerity of our motives, in our just and right intentions.

Again, we should have faith in God's respect for us. It is not humility to call ourselves "worms of the dust." We are men and women. We are sons of God. We are somebody. We are worthy of God. Jesus said, "They shall walk with me in white for they are worthy" [Rev. 3:4]. To be sure there is a standpoint from which we should consider ourselves unworthy and unprofitable. That is not an attitude of self-depreciation. It is only recognizing our human situation. Nevertheless that is only part of the truth. We have wonderful possibilities. We are wonderful beings. God counts us worthy to stand in his presence before his throne. There is therefore no need that we should go through life in sackcloth and ashes bewailing what we are. We should recognize that God respects us and esteems us. He would not have sacrificed his Son for us had this not been true.

73.

We should have faith in our Christian experience. I have seen many downcast, doubting people. When I asked them what was the matter, some said, "I don't feel right." When I asked, "Why don't you feel right?" some answered, "I don't know, but I don't feel right." You may have the same experience. Perhaps you don't feel right. Well, what of it? Your emotions are not the test of your spiritual state. Some people feel bad physically when there is very little wrong with them, perhaps nothing of any consequence. Others may feel all right when they are in the grasp of a deadly disease. Just so spiritually. You cannot tell by your emotions what is your relation with God. Your emotions were never intended to be evidences of your spiritual standing. We must stand by faith, learn to exercise faith, learn to live by faith. Judge yourself righteously. Do not let your feelings master your faith. Make your faith master your feelings. As a general thing, when you believe right you will feel right, but very often people base their faith on feelings instead of on realities. It does not matter so much how you feel. How are you? This is to be settled by your faith quite apart from your feelings, and when you settle it, leave your feelings out of the question as evidence.

We should make a practice of building into our lives every day the building blocks of faith; not building blocks of doubts and fears, anxieties, and worries. Plenty of these building blocks of faith are to be had. In learning to build with blocks of faith, we learn the secret of the singing heart, of a joyful, happy Christian experience, of certainty for the future and for the present.

Singing in the Quietness

No life is so sheltered but it has times of distress and difficulty and ofttimes of conflict and turmoil. But no life need be so full of these that there is no time for quietness.

No one fights all the time. No one works all the time. For every soul there is time for withdrawal from all the activities of life, a time to rest in quietness.

Life in this age is intense. People live so much in the public that many feel they have no time for quietness. Others are so disturbed in their minds, so constantly under a strain, they are so continually facing real or imaginary difficulties, that they have no rest of spirit. God does not want us to miss the quiet side of life. He wants us to be able to sing the songs of quietness that differ from all other songs. Before we can sing these songs we must become quiet and enter into a place of restfulness.

Here is a promise: "Whoso hearkeneth unto me shall dwell safely, and shall be quiet from fear of evil" (Prov. 1:33). Isaiah, prophesying of the coming gospel age, said: "The work of righteousness shall be peace; and the effect of righteousness quietness and assurance forever. And my people shall dwell in a peaceable habitation, and in sure dwellings, and in quiet resting places" (Isa. 32:17-18). It. is our privilege to have this blessed experience.

The effect of righteousness is certain. It does not bring turmoil or anxiety, but quietness and assurance. The first thing to make sure of therefore is that we are righteous. We may count ourselves unrighteous or we may count ourselves righteous. The important thing is—how does God count us? If we have been saved by his grace, if we have been washed from our sins in the precious blood of his dear Son, if we have been born again, we are righteous. If we are living in obedience to God to the best of our understanding, if we are living in humility and trust, sincerely endeavoring to do his will, we are righteous.

There is a difference between being righteous and being perfect. None of us will attain such a perfection in this world that we have no faults or shortcomings to be overcome. But righteousness, first imparted by God in salvation, is preserved as long as we preserve an attitude of submission to him, with a sincere purpose to please him as the ruling motive in our lives. But in order to have quietness and assurance we must believe that we are righteous. We must not always be questioning ourselves, always looking for flaws in ourselves, putting ourselves on the rack of torture. We must be fair to ourselves. We must have faith in ourselves. Then we can dwell in a peaceable habitation and in a quiet resting place.

Care, anxiety, fearfulness, are not from God. He has said, "I will give you rest" [Matt. 11:28]. Many people do not become quiet long enough to rest. Sometimes people feel they must be doing something all the time. Activity is proper, but persons in a certain state of super tension cannot sit down and be quiet. They have a constant impulse toward activity. I have known people who had to be compelled to sit down and sit quietly for a considerable time until their nerves relaxed. They had entirely lost control of themselves so that without the restraining forces of another they were unable to be quiet or to relax.

Sometimes we get into a similar condition spiritually. There is a continual inner restlessness, a something that cannot be satisfied. We become agitated and bothered. We worry and fret. We suffer a thousand fears of present and future ills and troubles. We need to come to quietness before God and to see him as he is and to submit to his will without reserve. We need to hear him say, "Be still and know that I am God" [Ps. 46:10]. Straining and struggling come from rebellion. Submission is the cure for this. If your life is in a turmoil, God's promise of rest is not being fulfilled in you. It is not God's fault. You are not giving him a chance. You may have that rest of soul by deliberately turning away from the thing that prevents your rest and diligently seeking the way that leads to quietness and peace.

Perhaps you need to disengage yourself from various useless and profitless activities. Perhaps you do not give any time to the cultivation of quietness. Quietness is something that must be learned. We need to learn how to say effectively to our spirit, as Jesus said to the waters, "Peace, be still" [Mark 4:39]. We need to learn how to relax our attention, to withdraw from our anxieties. We should learn to practice going into the secret closet, shutting the doors, closing everything out but God. The Scriptures speak of "the secret place of the Most High" [Ps. 91:1]. A writer said, "The secret place of the Most High is ever still, and if we dwell there our hearts will not be disturbed by any tumult without."

There is a way into this secret place. The strange thing about that way is that each of us must find it for himself. Most of us who do not find it do not look for it intently enough. We seem too busy. We should like to be in God's secret place, but we assume that under our circumstances we cannot be there. There is a road, and a short road, from wherever we are into God's secret place, that secret place of quietness and rest where he would commune with us and where our hearts can grow tranquil. To satisfy God and to satisfy our own hearts, we must be alone with God in his secret place.

The tempestuous surge of our emotions must be quelled. The tumult of spirit must be brought to quietness. Only then may we enter into that tender fellowship and delightful association with the Lord that it is his will for all Christians to have. W. G. Murray crowds a great deal of truth into a few words when he says, "Inner serenity becomes outward strength." We sometimes wonder why some Christians are so sure of themselves, why they seem to have such a sense of sufficiency to meet what may come. We wonder why they meet their circumstances with so little trepidation. In the midst of most severe tests they are serene and strong. The prophet said, "In quietness and in confidence shall be your strength" [Isa. 30:15]. We should give heed to learning this lesson.

We can cultivate a tranquil habit of mind. In Ezekiel's vision of the glory of God it is said of the living creatures, "When they stood, they let down their wings" (1:24). I once got a wonderful lesson from this saying. I stood upon a hilltop looking down into a valley. As I watched, a number of turkey buzzards alighted in the valley below me. Instead of folding their wings as buzzards usually do, they stood with them outstretched, looking about as though fearful of being attacked. They stood ready instantly to spring into the air. They made me think of many Christians who hold this constant attitude.

We should learn to let down our wings. We should learn how to rest. There may be clouds, even threatening clouds, upon the horizon of our lives. For the time being our sky may be entirely covered and shadows may darken the landscape as far as we can see. It takes only a small cloud to produce this effect. We may be tempted to think the whole earth is covered with shadow. We may let gloom sink into our souls. We should not do this. We should remember the truth expressed by Elizabeth Browning, "The blue of heaven is larger than the clouds." Tell yourself this over and over when you are tempted to be discouraged and remember that God has a way for you so that your heart may be quiet and free from fear and evil.

We have a place of refuge and that place of refuge is a quiet place, a place of safety and rest. A man was walking in the woods when he heard dogs baying. Presently a fawn appeared in sight. When it saw him it ran up to him and fell down at his feet and looked appealingly into his face. He fought off the dogs, took the fawn home, and raised it for a pet. If we should run to God in our troubles as confidently as that little fawn ran to the man, he would beat off our enemies and take us into a place of safety, calmness, and rest. We should have the simple faith that Whittier expresses in the lines,

I know not where His islands lift
Their fronded palms in air;
I only know I cannot drift
Beyond His love and care.

So often people ask, "How shall I get through the things that are ahead of me? How can I endure this?" The way to go through is to trust through. What do we do when we trust? What do you do when you trust the bank with your money? You just go about your business without worrying in the slightest degree as to the safety of your money. When you trust a friend you rely upon that friend. You do not question him. You believe in his loyalty to you. You take it for granted that everything will be all right between you. You do not expect anything unworthy of his friendship. You repose utmost confidence in him. It does not occur to you to question. You rest in full assurance in your friend or in your bank.

Trust removes every tendency to be disturbed. That is just the result when you trust God in that simple way. You rely upon him. You take it for granted that things will be all right because you are God's and God is looking after you. Your interests are safe in his hands, and therefore they must come out all right. Trusting him thus you enter into the rest of faith and from that rest of faith you sing the songs of quietness and of confident assurance.

The songs we sing in quietness are not the songs of battle, not the songs of the army camp, not the songs of the march. They are the songs of holy fellowship, of divine comradeship. They are the songs of the satisfied soul. Let us therefore adopt that attitude of soul toward ourselves, toward God, and toward life and all it may hold, that will bring us into the quietness and rest and tranquillity of the secret place of the Most High. Let us learn to sing the songs of quiet rejoicing, the songs of those who lie down beside the still waters.

Singing in Activity

Activity is a law of life. Life in the body continues only so long as there is activity of function. Soul rest does not imply stagnation. Rest is the result of the soul's attitude toward and relation with the spiritual, mental, and physical universe. It is one's adaptation to one's environment that produces harmony that prevents discord and friction.

When the machinery of life is well oiled it runs smoothly. It is not needful that we withdraw ourselves from the activities of life or shut ourselves up in a convent or cloister in order to have soul rest. We can mingle in life's activities; we can fully do our part and yet have that inner rest that brings calmness, peace, and satisfaction. These qualities are not the result of inactivity. They are not the result of death but of life, and often the most active and vigorous life is the one that is most restful. Activity begets a mental attitude that naturally bursts forth into song. It produces soul vigor as it does mental and physical vigor. Vigor creates energy. Energy finds its normal expression in activity. Activity produces satisfaction and gratification. These are expressed in rejoicing.

Lack of activity is the source of many troubles. Lack of proper physical exercise causes the muscles to grow flabby, the various bodily functions to grow sluggish, and creates a disposition toward further inactivity. It is also the cause of many diseases. It weakens the body and leaves it a prey to destroying germs. The man who does not use his mental faculties so as to keep them keen soon does not want to think; it is a task for him to think, and he will not think if he can avoid it.

The same laws apply to the spiritual being. The less active we are in spiritual things the less inclined we are to be active. The longer we are inactive the less power to be active we have. A great many people are weak and powerless Christians because they are inactive Christians. They are unable to meet the difficulties of life and overcome them readily because of the weakness induced by their lack of spiritual exercise. Every one of us should be active. It is the only way to develop spiritual vigor and strength. It is the only way to be a happy, rejoicing Christian.

Our activities, however, should be of a proper sort. There are many religious activities that build us up and strengthen us, that bring out our good qualities and develop them. Other religious activities produce an evil effect. Any activity that places the body under an undue strain, uses up too much nervous energy, or robs the body of its vitality results in hurt to the body.

In like manner religious excitement, extremism, and unbalanced enthusiasm, such as we see in some religious movements today, are distinctly hurtful to the soul. These have an effect upon the soul such as stimulants have upon the body. There must always be a reaction from them. That reaction is distinctly harmful. We should see to it therefore that our religious activities are wise activities, not the result of fanaticism or extremism, not unbridled enthusiasm or animal excitement. Our activities should be sane, moderate, reasonable, and within the bounds of Christian propriety.

There is nothing that will give zest to life like a great purpose. Too many lives merely drift. The Christians outstanding on the pages of history were all inspired with a consuming purpose to accomplish some service. Jesus went about doing good. He was under the urge of a great love. Notwithstanding all the opposition of those who should have been his helpers he rejoiced in spirit. Jesus was devoted to an ideal. That ideal was to uplift and save men. In the strength of that ideal he never faltered.

You and I need such an ideal. We, too, need the urge of a great love, a love for humanity. A multitude of opportunities abound for doing good. The heart of the world is longing for love and comfort, for kindly deeds, for helpfulness and mercy. What are we doing to supply this need? How much devotion have we? Let us note the devotion of Paul. He poured himself out to people, not only to his own nation, but to strangers, to those who had no natural claim upon him. He counted not his life dear unto himself that he might accomplish the great purpose that inspired him. It was his activity, ceaseless, and self-forgetful, that enabled him to be exceedingly joyful in all his tribulations. It was that very activity that made him joyful.

Drifting always becomes monotonous. We may enjoy it for a time, but if we want really to enjoy ourselves we must "get our backs into it." There is a great difference between being weary as a result of labor and the feeling of weariness that comes from idleness. When I was growing up I lived in the country. Sunday was usually a weary day. I longed for its passing that I might get to work again, not because I cared so much for work but because mere idleness and inactivity could give no satisfaction to my youthful spirit. When one is weary from labor he can rest and enjoy resting. When one is weary from idleness rest has no charms.

Many weary Christians are weary from idleness. They let the days pass and perhaps use but a few moments, if any time at all, for spiritual development or exercise. They know there are unsaved people all around them, but they do nothing about it. They know there are sick to be visited, but they do not visit them. They find a convenient excuse for their idleness just as every physical idler does.

They know sorrowing hearts who need comforting and poor persons who need ministering to. There are scores of opportunities all about them, but they are not using them. Then they wonder why they do not make more spiritual progress, why their life is not more blessed. They wonder why they have so many trials and difficulties to meet and why they seem to have no spiritual energy.

They need not wonder. They know very well what the results would be should they do the same physically as they are doing spiritually. Why then should they be in doubt as to the cause of their spiritual state? So many say, "Oh, if I had more joy in my Christian life!" We may as well say, "Why do we not have more to eat on our tables?" when we refuse to spend money to buy it.

We can sing the joyous song of the reapers if we are reapers. We can rejoice in accomplishments if we accomplish something. But accomplishment means definite activity, properly directed. A great many people are very active in what they suppose to be religious work but may not be religious work at all. What do the things we do amount to from a spiritual standpoint?

Really religious activities use the spiritual, not the merely physical, faculties and powers. Really spiritual activity is entering into the needs of people in a helpful way, comforting those who need comfort, ministering to the poor, encouraging the discouraged, helping wherever help is needed. Such activities will start the song of joy in our own souls.

When we throw light upon the darkened pathway of a fellow traveler that light is reflected upon our own pathway. When we minister to others, we are ministered to. When we bring joy to the sad, joy comes to our own hearts. But the trivialities with which so many religious people occupy themselves can never bring soul satisfaction.

It is not the greatness of our labors but their purpose, the earnestness that we put into them, and the quality of our own desires that make them worthwhile. It is not the seeming importance of what we do but the spirit we put into the doing. We may never have opportunities such as some others have; we may never have a place of importance or authority. This need not in the least hinder us from being as active as those who have more responsibilities and seemingly more or greater opportunities. If we make the most of our opportunities, whatever they are, we shall be happy. Not how great the opportunity but how greatly we rise to it—not what others think of what we do but how much unselfish devotion we put into the doing of it determines its value in God's sight.

Devotion to a worthwhile cause always has abundant reward. Here is the secret of the singing heart. If you will learn this secret and put it into practice you may have a heart that breaks into song from the inward pressure of joy as naturally as the safety valve of a boiler blows off under the pressure of the steam. The pressure of the steam depends upon the fire; so the heat and energy of devotion and love in our souls may be fervent enough to produce constantly recurring and overflowing songs.

Some in their imagination picture heaven as a place of rest. They think we shall sit around and play on golden harps or leisurely stroll over golden streets. That is not my idea of heaven. I believe the law of life in heaven will be the same as it is upon earth; that is, that activity of a constructive kind will be necessary to happiness. I do not know what heaven is like. No doubt it is inexpressibly glorious, but my faculties are so limited in this world, my activities so bound by the restrictions and limitations of the body, that my soul longs for the opportunity for greater expansion of its powers.

There are boundless possibilities for development in every human being. There will be opportunities for this development in the world to come. That development will mean activity, not useless activity, but productive activity. It is written of that world, "His servants shall serve him" [Rev. 22:3]. The golden harps will sound and the singers will sing in heaven, not because they are rest-ing, not because they have nothing else to do, but because they are giving expression to those joys that result from their heavenly activities. After all, the harps and the singing, the golden streets, the gates of pearl, are only figures. They stand for spiritual realities that mean far more than are expressed in these feeble figures. We shall rest from our labors of this world not in inactivity but in action. Very often in this life the best sort of rest is activity of a different sort. Let us remember that whether in earth or heaven, the song of joy is born of activity.

Facing the Sunrise

Life is such that we may face either of two directions. The direction we choose to face determines to a large extent our happiness or lack of happiness. If we face westward we face the sunset. This means facing the fading light, the passing away of things. It means the coming of darkness. This is a changing world; much that is dear to us passes away. If we fix attention on our losses, darkness and gloom will settle upon us. We shall look upon fading hopes, empty chairs, blessings passed away. Facing this way tends to bring melancholy and sadness.

It is better to face the sunrise. Even in the darkness we may face the east with the assurance that dawn will presently come. There will be new friends for the old friends that are gone, new hopes for the perished ones, new opportunities instead of the vanished ones. Let us resolutely look away from the sunset to where the dawn will break again and the light shine anew upon us.

Facing the sunrise is an art; it must be learned. The natural tendency, especially with very many, is to face the sunset. It is the hopeful Christian who is the joyous Christian. He looks ahead for better things. He is not disappointed. The good is never all in the past. The lost treasure may be replaced. What the future brings us will in a great measure depend upon the way we meet it, the outlook we have toward it, and the faith with which we respond to it.

Let us change the figure somewhat. We should always face the light. When we face away from the light we walk in our own shadow. When we turn about and face the light the shadows are behind us. We need not walk in the shadows. It is our privilege to walk toward the light, to walk in the light, not in the darkness. Jesus said we should have the light of life and that we should not walk in darkness. There is a way, therefore, to have our pathway illuminated and our steps made sure. There is great value in the forward-looking attitude. One writer said, "It is worth a thousand pounds a year to have the habit of looking on the bright side of things." Note that he calls it a habit. It is just that. We can cultivate good habits as well as bad habits. We should deliberately cultivate the habit of looking on the bright side.

To look on the bright side of life we must have the right sort of ideals. High ideals are a great inspiration. The momentum imparted to the soul by great ideals will carry it through many places of difficulty and raise it above many obstacles.

The power of the ideal has been thus expressed, "Our ideals find us where we are; they carry us where we ought to be." Ideals, even if we never reach them, put a zest and vigor into life that it can have from no other source. Ideals help us to make the best that can be made of ourselves. Through ideals we aim high, we strive earnestly. In contemplation of our ideals we lost sight of much that we are the better for losing sight of.

One writer declares, "The best way to correct imperfection in ourselves and in others is constantly to emphasize ideals instead of punishing faults." Many people condemn themselves and feel that they ought to punish themselves for their faults. Just recently I had a letter, a part of which I will quote, to illustrate the attitude toward life and toward themselves many people have: "I cannot understand why it is that I cannot get complete victory. Perhaps it is self-condemnation. I am wondering if I do not enjoy condemning myself because I somehow think by going over all the ugly past and saying to myself, 'What if God won't forgive you?' or, 'Maybe God won't forgive,' I punish myself a little more, and perhaps God will take pity on me."

Such punishment is no part of God's plan for us. It in no way makes us more acceptable to him. It is, however, a great hindrance to us. The psalmist had learned his lesson. He said, "It is vain for you to rise up early, to sit up late, to eat the bread of sorrows" (127:2). The priests of Baal tried to gain the favor of their gods by cutting themselves and otherwise punishing themselves [1 Kings 18:28]. God's approval is not won in this way. He would have us trust in his mercy, look to the sunshine of his love, face away from the shadows toward the light. We should emphasize our ideals and reach forward to them, forgetting those things that are behind.

Sometimes people start in life with high ideals, but as the years go on they lose these high ideals. Then the high hopes that went with those ideals fade. People become disillusioned; they come to look upon the sordid and unlovely and forget that life has a better side. Their minds become indifferent to what once inspired them. We should beware of lowering our ideals or forgetting them. The pure always remains pure. The good is always good. Realities do not change. Our point of view may become wrong. We may come to face in the wrong direction. But the realities remain as they were. Youth is naturally idealistic. We should carefully preserve that idealistic outlook of youth and keep young in spirit. Years ago I observed people becoming old before their time, losing their ideals, becoming pessimistic. I resolved I would never become old. I said to myself, "My body may get old, my hair may grow white, but my spirit shall never grow old."

I was struck by the tone of a letter I received recently. The writer of it was telling her troubles. In it she said, "I am an old woman. I am fifty-four years old." It is tragic that one should view life thus. Old at fifty-four; think of it!

I know people who are young at eighty-five. Their hearts are young. Their outlook is young. Their idealism has not diminished. The way to keep young is to keep interested in life, to love people, to have faith in God.

A bright sunrise may be succeeded by a cloudy day. It is important that we know how to have sunshine on these cloudy days. There is just one way to do it. That is faith's way. Faith runs a shaft up through the clouds and lets the sunshine come down on the heart. In the natural world there is plenty of sunshine just above the clouds on the cloudiest day. In life there is likewise plenty of sunshine if through faith we rise above the clouds or if we pierce them and let the sunshine through.

Of course, we may so focus attention upon our troubles that we do not observe the sunshine. Maclaren says, "The secret of finding sunbeams in everything is simply letting God have his own way, and making your will the sounding board and echo of his." Yes, that is the real motive of joyful Christian living. To let God have his way without any reluctance or hesitation is one of the greatest secrets of the singing heart. God's will, when gladly submitted to, always brings joy. We rejoice to have his will done. It is shrinking from his will that causes the hurt and stills the song.

Very needful is the cultivation of a sense of humor. We need a safety valve. The faculty of mirth is given us as a safety valve. Sometimes tears serve a good purpose, but in general it is better to laugh over our troubles than to cry over them. The results physically, mentally, and spiritually will be better. Through a sense of humor we can sheer off much that is hard and troublesome. What we cannot sheer off we can make easier to bear. Many a person has kept up courage, faith, and determination through a good laugh and has broken the spell of defeat.

Humor, mirth, and playfulness are all divinely created to serve God's purpose in us, to balance the pain, the heartaches, and the tears that assuredly will come. The smiling countenance, the sparkling eye, the joyful laugh, add spice to life. They not only come from sunshine in the heart, but they produce more sunshine therein and all about. If we are inclined to be melancholy and troubled, moody, and heavyhearted, we need to fill the other side of the scales with joy. We may make life surrender its treasures of gladness and cheer. It has such treasures for us all, but sometimes we have to set ourselves to find them.

When I need supplies for my work I fill out a requisition for them and send it to the proper place. All I need is in stock, but none of it comes to me until I ask. No doubt many of our blessings grow shelf-worn waiting for us to seek them, "Ye have not, because ye ask not" (Jas. 4:2). Jesus said, "Ask and it shall be given you; seek and ye shall find" [Matt. 7:7]. We should ask and seek of God, of life, of circumstances, till we are enriched, with joy and peace and true happiness.

It is our right to be happy. We owe it to ourselves, and life owes it to us that we be happy. Life will pay us all it owes us if we give it a fair chance. But to receive what is ours we must face the sunrise where these things are, not the sunset where they are not.

Victorious Living

I sing because I'm happy,
I sing because I'm free;
His eye is on the sparrow,
And I know He watches me.

The song of victory is a song of faith. In reality every song is a song of faith. Faith is the basis of happiness. It is the inspiration of song. We return to the theme of faith here because faith is central and vital. Christian faith is what makes the Christian life so joyous. Many who call themselves Christians are not joyous. That is because they do not have an active faith. Paul was radiantly joyful solely because he was a man of deep and settled faith and had the assurance that comes from such a faith. We quote his words, "The life that I now live in the flesh I live by the faith of the Son of God" [Gal. 2:20].

To Paul, Christ was real. His relations with Him were real. On that stormy sea journey that ended in shipwreck Paul could say to those in danger with him that all would be well, that not a life would be lost. He could speak confidently because the angel of the Lord had stood by him and had given him the assurance of faith.

God promised, "My presence shall go with thee" [Ex. 33:14]. That promise has been a comfort and consolation to God's people for three thousand years. We need to cultivate a sense of God's presence. He has said, "I will never leave thee, nor forsake thee" [Heb. 13:5]. His presence with us is real whether or not we can realize it. We need not try to create a sense of its reality in our imagination. It is a fact, not a fancy. We have only to sense the fact and to treat it as a fact. We may say that God is everywhere. True, but it is not his presence everywhere that counts for us; it is only that part of everywhere where we are. God is just as real in that little part of everywhere where you and I now are as he is in heaven on his throne. It is his presence where we are that really counts for us. Therefore it is the sense of the reality of his presence with us that makes him real to us.

The psalmist said, "Thou art with me" [Ps. 23:4]. To be able to say this means much. First of all it means safety. The story of how one of God's children came to realize her safety in the abiding presence of God is told by Hannah Whitall Smith:

> I was attending a prayer meeting when a poor woman rose to speak, and I looked at her wondering what she could say, little thinking she was to bring a message to my soul. She said she had great difficulty in living the life of faith on account of the second causes that seemed to control nearly everything that concerned her. Her perplexity became so great that she began to ask God whether he was in everything or not.
>
> After praying for a few days she had what she described as a vision. She thought she was in a perfectly dark place and that there advanced toward her from a distance a body of light which gradually surrounded and enveloped her and everything about her. As it approached a voice seemed to say, 'This is the presence of God.' While surrounded with this presence all the great and awful things of life seemed to pass before her—fighting armies, wicked men, raging beasts, storms and pestilences, sin and suffering of every kind.
>
> She shrank back at first in terror, but she soon saw that the presence of God so surrounded and enveloped each one of these that not a lion could reach out his paw nor a bullet fly through the air except as his presence moved out of the way to permit it, and she saw that let there be ever so thin a sheet, as it were, of this glorious presence between herself and the most terrible violence not a hair of her head would be ruffled nor anything touch her unless the presence divided to let the evil through. It was so also with the small and annoying things of life. Her difficulty vanished.

Her question was answered forever. God was in everything and the angel of his presence saved her.

We shall not all have such experiences to cause us to realize the presence of God and our safety therein. God has other ways of assuring us. We may greatly help by assuring ourselves continually that God is with us. If we should say to ourselves in our times of difficulty or danger, "God is with me; I am safe," we would presently come to feel safe no matter what the circumstances. If we should repeat over and over to ourselves in our times of need, "God is with me; God will help me," it would come to be a reality with us. It is real whether or not we realize it, but it profits us in our consciousness only when we realize it.

In times of storm we especially need to realize the sheltering presence of God. We can do much toward cultivating a state of mind that makes God's presence real in our dark times. We must not wait for the dark times to begin this development. We should practice the consciousness of God's presence until it becomes real to us at all times.

The sense of God's presence is sometimes vivid and strong. At other times we know God is near only by faith, therefore the need of cultivating a sense of his presence by faith. Our faith will be tested with respect to this as with other things. The more tests faith meets and endures, the more it grows.

We need to learn to use our faith. We should form the habit of daily accomplishing something by our faith. We should pray every day the prayer of faith for some definite request. We cannot do this if we scatter our prayers too much. We can have a general faith that takes in all our needs and this we can exercise daily, but we need a particular exercise of faith to receive particular help and grace. We should pray for many things, but there are some things on which we should specialize. We should make them a special object of prayer. We should choose something that we feel to be the will of God for us. Then we should pray for that until it is granted, until faith grasps its objects and makes it a reality.

When we pray for many things but do not exercise definite faith for any one of them we weaken rather than strengthen our faith. Every day many circumstances large and small call for the exercise of faith. Little acts of faith build character and bring success and happiness.

Every exercise of faith prepares us the more easily to exercise it next time. Every recognition of the power of faith and its accomplishments makes us more capable of faith. The exercise of faith in the daily routine gives us a sense of God's partnership with us, of his continuous help. Sometimes we realize very greatly our need of help. Do we realize God's willingness to give that help, and do we act upon such a realization? It has been said that God helps those that help themselves, but I think God loves best to help those who cannot help themselves. I think that those who are faint and weak with the toils of life and those whose courage falters may more than any others have cause to believe that God will help them. God is not looking for opportunities to help those who need no help. His help is for those who stand in need of it and who must have it. To such it is freely given when they trust him.

So many say, "Oh, if I knew how to have faith!" One thought may help you. Never let what you do know be weakened by what you don't know. Stick to what you do know. Always remember that God's promises and your experience with him are facts. Nothing can change them. Your fears and uncertainties do not change God's love. So settle down on God's promises. Do not doubt them. Do not question them. Rely upon them. Leave the unknown to God. Stand upon the known while you face the unknown.

James said we should show our faith by our works. If we believe in God, we ought to act like it. "He thinks he believes it, but he doesn't," said a woman of a man who had been professing his faith in the gospel. "If he really thought he had a friend like that, rich enough and strong enough to help him in every trouble and willing to do it, too—somebody who is sending him blessings all the while he is here and getting a beautiful home prepared for him to use afterward—do you suppose he would go about so gloomy and discouraged all the time?" Assuredly not. Our conduct is in harmony with what we truly believe. So, if we really believe God's promises we shall be joyful Christians.

We should truly believe and have the will to put that belief into our deportment. We should have the will to be cheerful, bright, and pleasant. We should keep our troubles out of our eyes, out of our voices, and out of our movements. We should not advertise that we have trouble. The more we allow our physical attitude, the tones of our voice, and the look in our eyes to depict discouragement, defeat, or uncertainty, the more we shall have within to overcome. God meant us to be victorious, so let us adopt the attitude of victory and say, "Since God meant me to be victorious I mean to be victorious. It is my right to be victorious. Through God's help I will be victorious. I am victorious." This attitude will go far toward making us victorious and toward making us realize our victoriousness.

There are times when our faith grows weary, when we find faith difficult to exercise. After long effort, we may say, "My faith is worn out." At such times we may find it difficult to pray. At such times people are inclined to mistrust their own experiences and question whether they are entirely right with God. Alice E. Worcester tells what she does under such circumstances.

When I am very weary
I do not try to pray;
I only shut my eyes, and wait
To hear what God will say.

At times we can only hold still and wait. At such times that is all God requires of us. That is all that is necessary. If God does not speak when we wait to hear him speak we may be sure that he will speak when it is needful for him to speak, and when he speaks he will cause our hearts to rejoice. in these times of weariness we should not let down our faith. We should rest in faith.

We have said that faith brings joy. Over in Africa on the Congo River stands a native village. Formerly its inhabitants were sunk in ignorance, and they lived in mud huts that abounded in filth. A missionary went to the town and proclaimed the gospel message. They heard, believed, accepted it, and were saved. They were transformed and set about the transformation of their town. To celebrate the great change that had come they changed the name of the town, and now it is known as Joy Town. Christ can make our town, any town, Joy Town to us.

Let us not forget that what life is depends upon what we are, and what we see depends upon how we look. An old fable goes like this: "A cold firebrand and a burning lamp started out one day to see what they could find. The firebrand came back and wrote in its journal that the whole world was dark. It did not find a place wherever it went in which there was light. The lamp came back and wrote in its journal, 'Wherever I went it was light.' What was the difference? The lamp carried its light with it and illuminated everything. The dead firebrand had light and everywhere it went everything was dark.

To sum up our thoughts, the secret of the singing heart consists in learning to be what we ought to be and in holding the attitude we ought to hold toward life. It consists in learning to adjust course to our circumstances and to be happy in those circumstances. It means to take advantage of favorable circumstances that come, to make best of the here and now, and to look forward to future with confident expectation of success with determination to have success. It consists of walking with God, believing in him, and acting on that belief day by day. Doing this we shall be blessed. We shall have joy and happiness, and "sorrow and sighing shall flee away" [Isa. 35:10].